Time Bomb in the Church

Time Bomb in the Church

Defusing Pastoral Burnout

Daniel Spaite, M.D.

with Debbie Salter Goodwin

Beacon Hill Press of Kansas City
Kansas City, Missouri

Printed in the
United States of America

Cover Design: Ted Ferguson

Library of Congress Cataloging-in-Publication Data

Spaite, Daniel, 1957-
    Time bomb in the church: defusing pastoral burnout / Daniel Spaite with Debbie Salter Goodwin.
        p. cm.
    Includes bibliographical references.
    ISBN 0-8341-1764-9 (pbk.)
    1. Clergy—Job stress. 2. Clergy—Psychology. 3. Burn out (Psychology)—Religious aspects—Christianity. I. Goodwin, Debbie Salter. II. Title.
    BV4398.S63   1999   99-18663
    248.8'92—dc21   CIP

10   9   8   7   6   5   4   3   2   1

To Dana, my wonderful wife of 20 years . . .
whose prayers and prodding
made this book possible.
And to my dad . . .
a faithful pastor
and unwavering minister
of the gospel.

Contents

CHAPTER 1

A Time Bomb Ticks

There is a time bomb ticking in the church. It hides in the most unlikely place. It does its most damage in total camouflage. When ready to explode, it can destroy a single person or a whole family or seriously injure a church. Is it a satanic conspiracy? A liberal avalanche? New Age subtleties? Marriage infidelity? While each of these is a serious problem facing the church, the time bomb that ticks is even more elusive because it wears the clothes of the time-honored work ethic and respectable compassion.

What is this time bomb that ticks away with undetected certainty? It is the overworked, stressed-out lifestyle of the modern pastor. It is the work patterns and leisure deficits that leave a pastor spent with no backup for recovery. It is the contemporary anomaly called burnout.

What is this time bomb . . . ? It is the overworked, stressed-out lifestyle of the modern pastor.

The time bomb exploded in my family when I was a freshman in college. The phone interrupted my college routine with the news that my 43-year-old pastor father was in ICU, holding tenuously to life.

The Sunday before, the church had held the required pastoral vote.[1] My dad, mother, and we three children had experienced some anxiety because of some opposition in the church to my dad's leadership. In spite of the fact that the church had experienced positive spiritual and numerical growth, we feared the vote could mean a move for our family. He survived the vote, but the following Tuesday he experienced some dizziness and then collapsed. The next thing he knew, paramedics were at his side, inserting IVs and preparing him for transfer to the emergency room. Tests revealed he had serious internal bleeding.

Although his medical chart recorded "bleeding duodenal ulcer," even his doctor agreed that the full diagnosis should include chronic stress. Dad had pastored his present assignment for seven years. Within that time the church grew from 250 to 550 in worship. In addition, he was working to complete a doctorate, spending all his vacation time in classes and all his leisure time in study. Internal church tensions climaxed during the church's phenomenal growth. Relationship pressures, administrative overload, family responsibilities, the push for the doctor of ministry—all became contributing ticks in the time bomb.

My family was fortunate. The explosion was a warning. My dad recovered to pastor again. He faced the difficult issues of his out of balance lifestyle. His physical recovery would be as complete as his recovery from his chronically stressed lifestyle. He recognized that his call from God was not a call to burnout but to deliver "reasonable service" (Rom. 12:1, KJV).

The stark statistics reveal that pastors are leaving the ministry in epidemic proportions.

Some pastors understand the lesson too late. Some never learn it at all.

The stark statistics reveal that pastors are leaving the ministry in epidemic proportions. One Evangelical denomination recently reported that in a seven-year period, one-third of their pastors had left the ministry (excluding retirement and death).[2] A Focus on the Family survey to 5,000 pastors revealed that 40 percent of pastors have considered leaving their pastorates in the last three months![3]

Why All the Dropouts?

Pastors leave the ministry for a number of reasons. Some leave because they come to understand that they never had a call. They realize that their own ambition or the influence of others led them to become a pastor. A church, a family member, a friend, or even their own desires may have called them, but God did not. "No one takes the honor [spiritual leadership] to himself, but receives it when he is called by God" (Heb. 5:4). Thus, leaving a pastorate to follow God is never a failure. Obeying God always defines successful ministry.

Sometimes a minister leaves because God's call changes. Pastoring may identify a chapter in the life of God's servant. By God's sovereign design, a new call directs the minister to serve Him in another capacity. Haggai's story illustrates this biblical precedent. God called Haggai for a specific purpose and for a limited period. His recorded public ministry lasted only four months. However, in that brief period, Haggai encouraged the people who had returned to Jerusalem to continue rebuilding the Temple as God had directed. There is no reason to think that God has stopped calling servants for a specific ministry and for a specific time. However, the Bible reveals that this type of call is rare.

What of the rest who continue to understand God's call but still find it necessary to leave? Economic stresses, marriage or family problems may influence a pastor to leave. Catastrophic circumstances such as a life-threatening or life-altering illness contribute to decisions to leave. Certainly in-church tensions or a leadership standoff pushes more than one pastor to pack up the office and store his or her license. For most, it's a complicated mix of overwork and any of the aforementioned problems that lead to exhaustion, disillusionment, and eventually physical or emotional burnout.

The Time Bomb Ticks

Why are so many leaving when they were "not sent from men, nor through the agency of man, but through Jesus Christ, and God the Father" (Gal. 1:1)? How many pastors reach a point in their life when God wants to do His greatest work through them but are unable to participate in those great victories because of physical, mental, or spiritual exhaustion? How many, at the brink of seeing great revival for which they may have been praying for years, miss the spiritual renewal because of debilitating diseases associated with overwork?

The time bomb ticks! It waits to destroy God-called leaders or at least reduce the effectiveness of their ministries by forcing them into survival mode. It ticks imperceptibly at first. By the time a pastor hears the unwelcome warning, it may be too late.

Not Me!

You may be thinking, "I'm already under pressure, and I don't want to read about stress." However, the focus of this book is not to talk about stress but to equip you to identify harmful patterns and prevent burnout.

On the other hand, you may say, "I know some stressed-out pastors, but I certainly am not one of them." Whether you perceive your risks or not, you should recognize that the very nature of professional ministry today tends to engulf the pastor in a sea of stressful circumstances. The direct result of this reality has led George Barna to say: "We appear to be losing many pastors after relatively brief careers in full-time ministry."[4]

Other researchers conclude that there are "startling numbers of clergy . . . who are prematurely terminating their careers due to burnout."[5] Clearly, these findings result from the physical, emotional, mental, and spiritual tensions that the ministry lifestyle inflicts on many, if not most, ministers of the gospel.

Like Emergency Medicine

In my vocation as a medical doctor specializing in emergency medicine, I witness a society coming apart at the seams! As the director of the Emergency Department in a university Level I trauma center, I have a unique view of the crumbling foundations of this generation. Often I simply scrape people up and put them back together so that they can shoot each other again. However, I profoundly feel the call of God to the ministry of medicine. That call pushes me to look for opportunities to encourage patients to a life of wholeness beyond the emergency room. Many times I care for multiple people with major trauma all at once. Some people object when I place someone else's emergency before theirs. However, my job requires me to prioritize.

The ministry of the modern pastor seems strangely similar to what I do. Today's pastors also witness the crumbling foundations of society's most basic unit: the family. Ministering to such needs, they must learn to manage one emergency after another. They finish caring for one person in crisis just in time for the next one to appear. While the goal of pastoral care goes beyond physically putting people back together again, that goal often nose-dives while hurting people repeat the same hurtful patterns, leaving a pastor feeling ineffective.

Unlike my emergency room responsibilities, you are deeply committed to life past the crisis. As a minister of the gospel, you tackle situations with eternal implications. It comes from the call, but it contributes unnumbered ticks to the time bomb.

Firsthand Experience

My profession significantly impacts both the perspective and the content of my understanding of the ticking time bomb. Medical training and practice give me insight I use to lead others to physical and mental health. However, the message about the time bomb does not come from medical experience alone. It comes from my heart and firsthand experience.

I grew up in a pastor's family and thank God that, by His grace, my parents enjoyed a long and fulfilling ministry. Fortunately, our family did not suffer any of the devastating consequences that many who live in a pastor's "glass house" experience. My brother is a pastor, and my sister is a nurse specializing in diabetes management. All three of us have found great fulfillment in loving others to Christ. However, we did experience firsthand the pressures that the church places on the pastoral family. There were the family vacations we cut short because of a death in the church. There were long hours and too many evenings when Dad left us for someone else's emergency. No child will ever understand why people say bad things about his or her parent, even under the cover of good intentions. Church votes only made negative undercurrents more public. When the ministry tug came before a family tug, it created stress for everyone in the family.

Medical Knowledge Makes Biblical Sense

In the past decade, I have diligently endeavored to become a student of the Word. This has helped me to properly integrate my medical experience into a biblical view of life, health, and ministry. I have come to understand that the Bible speaks clearly to stress and overwork as well as their impact on the body. During this journey with God, I have sensed a growing urgency to give this message to today's pastor. I want to deliver more than a warning. I want to offer practical ways to help the pastor personalize these principles.

Responding to the Time Bomb

When someone reports an object with mysterious ticks, emergency measures begin. Bomb-sniffing dogs and those trained in defusing explosives work to identify and disarm a potential catastrophe. Who works to defuse the time bomb of pastoral burnout in the church today? How many more casualties will fall before we take early measures to defuse the bomb?

How many more casualties will fall before we take early measures to defuse the bomb?

In response to this time bomb, this book calls the shepherds of the church to a life of inner peace and serenity that our Master enjoyed and modeled during His time on earth. It is a plea and a plan to avoid becoming a casualty of the time bomb in the church.

We cannot wait. The time bomb ticks!

WHAT ABOUT YOU?

- **Can you identify a time bomb ticking in anybody around you?**

- Are you aware of stress factors that could be the ticks of a time bomb?

- Have you ever considered leaving the ministry?

ENDNOTES

1. This denominational requirement has since changed to involve a less public pastoral review.

2. Wilbur Brannon, Pastors' Leadership Conference, San Diego, August 9, 1995.

3. H. B. London and Neil B. Wiseman, *Pastors at Risk* (Wheaton, Ill.: Victor Books, 1993), 25.

4. George Barna, *Today's Pastors* (Ventura, Calif.: Regal Books, 1993), 40.

5. M. L. Morris and P. W. Blanton, "Denominational Perceptions of Stress and the Provision of Support Services for Clergy Families," *Pastoral Psychology* 42 (1994): 348.

CHAPTER 2

A Land Mine: The Hidden Impact of Stress

How many times it will happen, no one knows. A child walks in the familiar area he or she calls home and takes one step in the wrong place. What had been solid, ordinary ground explodes and takes parts of the body, or even his or her life, with it. We call the hidden explosive a land mine because it hides below the ground, ready to detonate from the slightest pressure. Today, international attention focuses on raising awareness and funds for land mine recovery. The goal? To prevent future blasts. To save people from unsuspected death and dismemberment.

It is time to look for land mines closer to home. While they are not constructed with chemicals, powders, or wires, they rest below the surface of a pastor's life and explode with unsuspected destruction. Stress is the land mine I am describing. Stress has the potential to do as much damage to a life and family as a land mine explosion in Vietnam. So why is there no public outcry against this damaging intruder?

Because the negative effect of stress can occur without anyone suspecting the severity of its impact. We see a good example of this in research showing the impact of "life change events" on health. These investigations uncover a clear link between stressful events in life and the occurrence of disease. Several rating tools exist. Most ask you to use the list to select life events that you have experienced in the last 12 months. While there are several sophisticated mathematical tools for scoring, research studies demonstrate that the best evaluation is not a score but the total number of changes in life events.

Look at the examples from the Social Readjustment Rating Scale (Table 1). Notice that not all entries are negative. Life stressors include positive events like getting married, reconciling marital problems, retirement, pregnancy, changing work, outstanding personal achievement, vacations, and Christmas. What the scale points out is that change, any change, produces stress, even when it is something as positive as going on a vacation. Therefore, it becomes difficult to sort through the negative effects from stress when both positive and negative stresses contribute. This reminds us that many aspects of life negatively impact us, even when we are unaware of their effects.

This is certainly true of our bodies, as examples from the cardiovascular system will show.

TABLE 1: THE SOCIAL READJUSTMENT RATING SCALE[1]

1. Marriage
2. Troubles with the boss
3. Detention in jail or other institution
4. Death of spouse
5. Major change in sleeping habits
6. Death of a close family member
7. Major change in eating habits (amount of food or change in meal hours)
8. Foreclosure on a loan
9. Revision of personal habits (dress, manners, associations, etc.)
10. Death of a close friend
11. Minor violations of the law
12. Outstanding personal achievement
13. Pregnancy
14. Major change in the health of family member
15. Sexual difficulties
16. In-law troubles
17. Major change in number of family get-togethers
18. Major change in financial status
19. Gaining a new family member

20. Change in residence
21. Child leaving home
22. Marital separation
23. Major change in church activities
24. Marital reconciliation
25. Being fired from work
26. Divorce
27. Changing to a different line of work
28. Major change in the number of arguments with spouse
29. Major change in responsibilities at work
30. Wife beginning or ceasing work outside the home
31. Major change in working hours or conditions
32. Major change in usual type or amount of recreation
33. Taking on a mortgage
34. Taking on other major loans
35. Major personal injury or illness
36. Major business readjustment
37. Major change in social activities
38. Major change in living conditions
39. Retirement from work
40. Vacation
41. Christmas
42. Changing to a new school
43. Beginning or ceasing formal schooling

A Heart Example

The heart is a muscle that pumps blood to the body. Because it has such high-energy requirements, a large amount of blood must flow to the heart muscle, or it cannot continue its normal function. The arteries that supply blood carrying oxygen and glucose to the heart muscle are called *coronary arteries.*

No one disputes that one of the major diseases in the American population is *coronary artery disease.* As this disease develops, plaques, or collections of fatty material, begin to build up. This process is called *atherosclerosis.* Early in this process, the heart is able to function normally. However, there comes a point when a critical narrowing of the coronary artery causes inadequate blood flow to the heart muscle. When this happens, a person often experiences chest pain.

Stress Can Restrict Coronary Blood Flow

In some people, muscle fibers in the wall of an artery will contract, causing a temporary narrowing, called a *vasospasm. Coronary artery vasospasm* occurs most frequently in people with *coronary artery disease.* However, some who have absolutely no evidence of plaque buildup in the coronary arteries will still experience a mysterious narrowing. What causes it? Medical research reveals that *emotional stressors,* or stress-producing events, may directly or indirectly cause this dangerous narrowing.

Another dramatic finding involves what is called *myocardial ischemia.* This occurs when the blood supply to the heart muscle is inadequate to meet the demand. This can occur without physical exertion. Stressful experience by itself can lead to *myocardial ischemia.* Research shows that doing things like mental arithmetic, or even reading a book, can cause a coronary blood supply problem in some people. Rozanski made the surprising discovery that public speaking can cause abnormalities in the heart's pumping function that are just as pronounced as those produced by physical exertion.[2] Researchers Deanfield and associates discovered an even more dramatic finding. They found that people with *myocardial ischemia* only experienced chest pain 25 percent of the time when stress was the underlying cause.[3]

Stress Can Interrupt the Heart's Rhythm

An electrical impulse travels through heart muscle fibers to initiate a beat that causes the heart to pump blood. Many factors can cause a misfire creating an irregular rhythm or *arrhythmia.* Abnormal heart rhythms can occur in people who have no evidence of coronary artery disease. Intense emotion, passing from sleep to wakefulness, performing mental arithmetic, or public speaking: all can cause an irregular heartbeat. Furthermore, an irregular rhythm can occur in some people who don't perceive even a hint that the heart is working abnormally.

So What?

Narrowed arteries, restricted blood flow, and irregular heart rhythm—what does this have to do with the pastor? Medical research shows that these cardiac problems can occur with nonexertive activities *and without any noticeable symptoms.* If public speaking could bring about an *arrhythmia,* then what about preaching, counseling, board meetings? What about regular ministry activities where stress shows up on the inside but not on the outside?

Second Cor. 4:16-18 reminds us that our bodies continue to decay even under normal circumstances and even when we have no awareness of the decay. Everyday life activities, even when they are not associated with any noticeable symptoms, may cause irregular rhythms, heart muscle dysfunction, and blood flow restrictions. Scientific research makes it clear that a lot happens in our bodies without our knowing it and no matter how we feel.

The Adrenaline Response

An important but hidden process is our built-in physical response to stress. Laboratory experiments using animals have studied this response to help us understand the impact of stress. One such study evaluated adjustment to stress. When animals repeatedly experience stressful events, they become *habituated.* That means that they adjust or adapt to the stressor. Repeated stress reduces *perception* of the stress. Eventually, it may no longer be perceived as a stress but as a *regular* part of life. What seems benign on the surface introduces a hidden problem. To deal with stress, the body produces stress hormones. The most familiar is *adrenaline.* However, with repeated stress, the body dramatically decreases its production of this stress hormone, while it increases the production of other stress hormones, such as *corticosterone.*

The animal stress studies show that an animal recognizes

when its adrenaline levels go up or down. You don't have to read medical research to know that. An adrenaline rush causes flushing, increased heart rate, and a general sense of tenseness. On the other hand, animals are *completely unaware* of any changes in corticosterone levels because this stress hormone doesn't cause any noticeable symptoms. Thus, when the adrenaline response decreases, the animal feels as if the stress has abated when, in fact, the animal has actually adapted to the presence of the stress. The problem is that the other non-symptomatic stress hormones, such as corticosterone, continue to increase. This places the animal in jeopardy due to being unaware of remaining in "stress mode." This and many other imperceptible adaptive mechanisms create a physical situation with increased susceptibility to illness.

The corticosterone response is a perfect example because prolonged elevations of this hormone can cause high blood pressure and increase the risk of coronary artery disease. The reason this is so important is that a hormonal change that occurs without accompanying symptoms may be just as important in the genesis of disease as the ones that cause noticeable symptoms.

This medical research has serious implications for the pastorate. How many stressors do you experience in the course of a day, week, month, and year? How many stressors no longer produce noticeable symptoms, leading you to believe that you have positively adapted to stress? You may have adapted to them and minimized your adrenaline response. However, there can still be major physiological abnormalities going on in your body.

Stress-Induced Analgesia

In 1976 several laboratory investigators identified a phenomenon termed *stress-induced analgesia*. They found that, when rats received repeated electrical shocks, their perception of pain progressively decreased as the shocks continued. They became *analgesic* or completely unaware of the pain, in spite of the fact that the shocks continued.

A few years later, new research explained this analgesia when it discovered *endorphins* and other *neurohormones* in humans. The research revealed that the brain secretes a hormone that decreases the ability to sense pain. For decades, physicians were using morphine and other narcotic medications to dramatically decrease pain in patients. These narcotics function by connecting to the endorphin receptors, resulting in effective pain relief.

This mechanism is a major reason for the phenomenon of stress-induced analgesia. Subjected to a painful stimulus, the brain responds by secreting endorphins. This results in pain relief or analgesia. However, the endorphin system also responds in other types of stress besides pain. Endorphin release occurs in response to emotional stressors as well.

Ministry-Induced Analgesia

The phenomenon of stress-induced analgesia underscores the fact that, when you are under stress, you may not feel it. You may not recognize factors that produce stress, especially if they exist as a repeated part of your lifestyle. This holds significant implications for ministry-related stress. Let me give a practical example.

You probably set the date for your vacation well in advance to fit between the regular demands of the church calendar. The mad push it takes to get ready to leave makes you wonder if you can really afford to take the vacation. Besides, you don't even feel like going on a vacation. You'd rather be working. But you promised, so you make your lists, delegate like crazy, leave numbers, and promise to keep in touch.

After you've been gone a day or two, it hits. An overwhelming fatigue. It's an effort to keep up with the rest of the family. Sometimes you don't. You blame it on age or being out of shape or even a virus. Soon it's time to think about returning. Much to your surprise you don't experience that hard drive push to get back. In fact, though you won't admit it to anyone, the thought of getting back behind your desk and looking at your calendar and all the work you set aside for your return fills you with a sense of dread. And you begin to entertain thoughts that maybe God is telling you it's time to leave.

God may be trying to get a message across, but it's not about a change *of* assignment. It's about a change *in* your assignment.

The vacation example shows what happens when we adapt so well to the stress that it produces a *ministry-induced analgesia.* Living with constant, unrelenting stress overworks the endorphin system. The numbing effect from endorphins prevents you from perceiving stressful symptoms. You are unaware of the stress *until you leave the situation.*

What This Means to You and Your Church

This has profound implications for your church. Your people deserve a pastor who perceives reality clearly. They need a leader who is tuned to the threats that endanger you and your people. A stressed pastor, who does not perceive his own stresses, cannot provide the strong, focused leadership that God desires for His Church.

We should thank God that He has given us internal mechanisms that provide relief from stress. However, this mechanism is meant to protect us *for brief periods of time.* It should be a short-term answer, not a long-term pattern. Overworking the protection system ignores the presence of a land mine. Only by breaking the cycle does the body return to normal. That happens only by removing the stress or removing yourself from the stressful situation, at least for short periods of time.

Just because you do not perceive stress does not mean that stress is absent.

Never forget—just because you do not perceive stress does not mean that stress is absent. Like the land mine, the unperceived explosive waits to unleash its destruction. Many don't deal with stress issues until the land mine explodes as a heart attack or another medical diagnosis. For others, it becomes a slow glide into a series of health issues that may not threaten life but that certainly affect the quality of life.

Ill Health and Disease

There is a difference between the presence of disease and the absence of health. Disease means that there is an identifiable structural or cellular abnormality in one or more tissues or organs of the body. On the other hand, the absence of health, or *ill health*, does not necessarily require a diagnosis of disease. Symptoms of ill health include abnormalities in bodily functions such as sleep, digestion, eating habits, sex drive, bowel regularity, mood, or even the general sense of well-being. Any or all of these may be present, in spite of the complete absence of detectable disease. In addition, depression, anxiety, and other emotional disorders may also accompany ill health and can cause substantial disability. For that reason, it is important to look beyond identifiable disease and examine the far more pervasive problem of ill health.

Chronic Stress and Ill Health

The impact of ill health in America is enormous. As an emergency physician, I constantly see people in an outpatient setting who experience symptoms of ill health rather than a disease. Ill health increases health costs. In fact, health-care costs of patients suffering ill health are nearly *10 times greater* than that of the average population.[4]

> Health-care costs of patients suffering ill health are nearly 10 times greater than that of the average population.

The real problem is not a body system gone awry. The real culprit is chronic stress. For example, consider a tension headache. The symptom originates in one or more muscles of the head or face. However, the actual problem is not muscular. A muscle spasm may be causing the *symptom,* but there is nothing wrong with the muscle. Instead, the muscle acts as the body's warning signal to help the person identify that there is something wrong within the physical or emotional makeup.

Chronic stress causes more ill health than disease. A complete list of stress-related symptoms would be endless. However, I want to discuss some of the more common examples.

Some of them have relatively technical names. I will use the medical term so that anyone who has suffered from the problem will recognize it.

Before giving these examples, I must give a typical doctor's warning. *Do not try to self-diagnose.* Any of the symptoms described here can point to disease as well as ill health. For example, to assume that chest discomfort is simply a symptom of ill health rather than coronary artery disease would be a foolish, and possibly fatal, mistake. With that warning in mind, let's look at some examples of ill health.

Abdominal Symptoms

It has happened in my emergency department more than once. A patient writhes on the examining table with intense abdominal pain. After an initial exam, I order the tests needed to find the problem: X rays, blood work, and other diagnostic procedures. But the tests uncover no abnormality, no tumor, and no disease. After ruling out serious disease, I match the symptoms to a problem called *irritable bowel syndrome.* The cause? Chronic stress.

The medical profession has known for years that emotional stress can cause abdominal problems. One of these problems relates to abnormal muscle contraction in the gastrointestinal tract called irritable bowel syndrome. Often, stress creates the contraction that causes the symptoms. The most common symptoms patients experience in this syndrome are nausea, vomiting, abdominal pain, diarrhea, constipation, gas, and weight loss. Others complain of bloating, headaches, anxiety, panic attacks, depression, flushing, and backaches. These multiple symptoms demonstrate how this syndrome involves many body systems while the organs themselves are in good working condition. Abdominal symptoms from this syndrome can be so dramatic they warrant surgery, even though the actual problem is chronic stress. In my experience, such unnecessary surgery is rare. However, other procedures such as upper and lower GI studies, barium swallow, endoscopy, and colonoscopy are often necessary to rule out serious disease. That means that patients who do not have a significant intestinal disease may undergo expensive and potentially complicated tests, all because of chronic stress. It is a high price to pay for unrecognized stress.

Digestive Problems

Sometimes stress-induced digestive problems mimic ulcers and other serious disorders. *Gastritis, dyspepsia,* and *heartburn* can all be traced to chronic stress. The most common of these problems is heartburn. Nearly everyone has experienced this symptom at some time in his or her life. However, frequent heartburn is abnormal, especially if it is associated with nausea, bloating, or pain.

Gastritis, inflammation of the stomach, can also cause symptoms that are identical to symptoms *of peptic ulcer disease.* To rule out the serious disorder, patients often undergo diagnostic tests. Following such diagnostic procedures, only 40 percent are diagnosed with an ulcer.[5]

Another problem related to the digestive tract involves the esophagus, the muscular tube that connects the mouth to the stomach. During normal swallowing, the esophagus receives the food or liquid. It then uses rhythmic muscle contractions to squeeze the food down into the stomach. Symptoms that signal a problem with this normal action can be heartburn, a lump in the throat, painful or difficult swallowing, and chest pain. Overactivity of the esophageal muscles creates the symptoms when there is no problem with the esophagus itself. Again, the problem reflects the presence of underlying emotional distress.

Diffuse esophageal spasm, or DES as it is more commonly known, is another cause of chest discomfort and pain. The pain usually occurs behind the breastbone and perfectly mimics *angina pectoris,* a rather intense heart pain, or *acute myocardial infarction,* which most people call a heart attack. Painful or difficult swallowing also accompanies the attack, which often occurs immediately after a meal. The culprit is a muscle spasm within the esophagus that causes the symptoms, but stress usually triggers the spasm. One study revealed that 27 percent of patients with chest pain were actually suffering from a problem with the esophagus. However, since such symptoms can point to more serious disease, it is always important to see a doctor if you are having any chest discomfort.

Essentially everyone has intermittent episodes of *esophageal reflux*, the backup of acid into the esophagus from its normal location in the stomach. However, many people who experience chronic stress will have such large volumes of acid reflux that it results in heartburn, chest pain, or other symptoms. In some, the reflux becomes so significant that it can cause inflammation and scarring of the esophagus. In severe cases, this can even lead to esophageal cancer.

Abdominal and digestive symptoms are not the only problems chronic stress causes. The 20th-century lifestyle has introduced another complex syndrome called *fibromyalgia.*

Fibromyalgia

The word *fibromyalgia* is a Latin term meaning pain in the muscles and connective tissues. Actually, the name poorly defines a syndrome that represents a large number of clinical disorders. Those with fibromyalgia will suffer pain in various muscle groups: low back, shoulders, neck, head, or legs. Symptoms often include morning stiffness. Fibromyalgia is another stress-related syndrome that can mimic heart pain when it involves the chest wall muscles.

A researcher named Moldofsky made a dramatic finding in 1975 that connected the symptoms of fibromyalgia to abnormal sleep patterns.[6] This explains why fibromyalgia is so often associated with fatigue and chronic tiredness. However, since the primary symptom is muscle pain, the sleep disturbance often goes unrecognized.

Perhaps you have read about the controversy concerning whether the cause of fibromyalgia is actually a virus. The issue surfaced when some with the Epstein-Barr virus manifested a clinical problem called *chronic fatigue syndrome*, which mimics fibromyalgia in many respects. Whether these syndromes are the same, separate, or related remains an unanswered question. However, evidence strongly suggests that chronic stress may predispose a person to sleep disorders and immune suppression. Thus, it is possible that fibromyalgia and chronic fatigue syndrome are symptoms resulting from an interaction between stress, immune system dysfunction, and a viral infection. Even if stress isn't the cause, it contributes to the problem.

Panic Attacks

Panic attacks come in all sorts of packages. One of the most common manifestations is hyperventilation. It happens when a person breathes so rapidly as to exhale too much carbon dioxide. The attack can be quite frightening because it feels as if you can't breathe, which increases the panic and intensifies the attack. The symptoms can look very much like a coronary problem with shortness of breath, light-headedness, a fast or irregular heartbeat, or chest pain. Often numbness or tingling in the hands or feet accompanies the attack. Physicians frequently prescribe sedatives for patients who experience the hyperventilation syndrome. Although this may decrease the symptoms, it does not treat the underlying problem. Sedatives only mask the symptoms and hide the root issue: chronic stress.

As these examples demonstrate, the symptoms of ill health are often warning signs pointing to an unhealthy lifestyle. Sometimes it takes more than one warning to uncover the real cause. When the body has raised its warning flags to no avail, repeated stress from compounding physical and emotional issues may bring a person to what is popularly called burnout.

Burnout: Another Form of Ill Health

When medical researcher Selye evaluated how humans responded to a variety of stresses such as environmental exposure, hemorrhage, injury, terror, and strenuous work, he found that all participants perceived stressors as hardship, which led to exhaustion. After this initial response, the subjects adapted to the situations, both physically and emotionally. Thus, for a period of time, they became used to the stress. If the stressor never went away, the individual finally gave up.

Burnout . . . is not a failure of faith or character, courage or stamina.

Unfortunately, this cycle describes the ministry of many pastors today. At first they may perceive the ministry-related stress as a hardship. Continuing to work without decreasing or eliminating the stress causes the pastors to adapt to the stress so that they feel as if there is no stress. This lasts for a variable amount of time, depending upon the individual characteristics of the pastor, the family, and the ministry circumstances. Ultimately, however, they cannot tolerate the stress-producing hardship and will often give up or burn out. Although the pastors may not have any diagnosable physical disease, this physical or emotional collapse or both definitely describes ill health and dramatically impacts their relationships, work performance, and family.

Burnout doesn't happen overnight. It is not a failure of faith or character, courage or stamina. It is the body's protective mechanism pushed to its extreme. The gears grind to a halt. Everything inside a person shouts, "Enough!" Finally, the message registers, almost too late.

Chronic Stress and Disease

Chronic stress not only complicates the health-care front by causing and sustaining ill health but also causes disease. Many years ago it became apparent that emotional and physical stress can cause disease. Take the study of soldiers during World War II as an example. No one doubts that soldiers experience extreme stress. Statistics showed that the rate of diagnosed duodenal ulcers doubled in the United States Army during the war but returned to its previous level after the war.[7] I wonder what kind of statistic pastors on the front line of spiritual warfare would record.

The medical community has long known that stress from one's social and professional environment can directly impact the likelihood of succumbing to disease. High stress and major life change frequently precede deaths from heart disease and severe coronary artery disease. Other companions to stressful life circumstances are hypertension, abdominal problems including peptic ulcers, acute episodes of asthma, and even some types of *hyperthyroidism,* or overproduction of the hormone *thyroxine* by the thyroid gland. High scores on instruments evaluating stress and life change events have been linked with an increased likelihood of experiencing tuberculosis, stroke, and complications with pregnancy. Depression has been shown to suppress immune function. In fact, the combination of depression and anxiety surfaces as a major factor associated with abnormalities of the immune system. This issue certainly speaks to the ministerial family because depression and anxiety are common problems among pastors and their spouses.

A Land Mine for Sure

It's a land mine, this problem of chronic stress. Medical research, case studies, and my own personal experience underline the profound impact that stress has on the human body and mind. While few studies target pastors as a separate population to study these health issues, there is no reason to suspect that conclusions from the huge volume of stress-related research are irrelevant to the professional minister. God has not changed the physical processes in a pastor's body simply because He called him or her to preach! Nor does He protect the minister from consequences of chronic stress brought about by lifestyle and work choices, as a friend of mine recently discovered.

I Should Have Seen It Coming

"I should have seen it coming," my pastor friend admitted as he told me the diagnosis his hospital tests confirmed. The doctor had explained his physical problem, but as he looked at me, we both knew the diagnosis his chart would never carry. Stress. A snowball effect of evening meetings, critical administrative issues, disgruntled people, financial needs, not to mention the merry-go-round of family responsibilities had finally finished its downhill roll.

"I should have seen it coming," he repeated, defeat underlining every word.

"But you didn't," I told him, trying to give him permission to forgive himself. "And now the question is, what are you going to do about it?" We both knew that the answer to that question was as important as the medical prescription he would take home from the hospital.

It Takes More than Treating Victims

It's not hard to compare the consequences of chronic stress with a land mine explosion. Both can be buried for years, camouflaged by a normal-looking environment, only to detonate and leave its victim with some form of physical or emotional damage. To prevent land mine explosions, someone must remove the land mine instead of simply treating its victims. How much more important that is for pastors. Now is the time to recognize either a susceptibility to stress and its consequences or its possible involvement in other health issues. While it isn't easy to acknowledge and work through stress-producing situations, it offers much more security than continuing a course that could lead to a land mine explosion.

WHAT ABOUT YOU?

- **Are you ignoring stress-related health problems?**
- **Have you adapted so well to stress patterns that you no longer experience the initial symptoms of stress?**
- **Could you be a victim of *ministry-induced analgesia*?**

- Are you suffering from unnecessary symptoms of ill health caused by chronic stress and overwork?
- Is there a land mine in your future?

ENDNOTES

1. T. H. Holmes and R. H. Rahe, "The Social Readjustment Rating Scale," *J Psychosomatic Res* 11 (1967): 213-18.

2. A. Rozanski, et al., "Mental Stress and the Induction of Silent Myocardial Ischemia in Patients with Coronary Artery Disease," *New England Journal of Medicine* 318 (1988): 1005-12.

3. J. E. Deanfield, et al., "Silent Myocardial Ischemia Due to Mental Stress," *Lancet* 3 (1984): 1001-5.

4. G. R. Smith, R. A. Munson, D. C. Ray, "Patients with Multiple Unexplained Symptoms: Their Characteristics, Functional Health, and Health Care Utilization," *Arch Int Med* 146 (1986): 69-72.

5. A. W. Williams, et al., "Investigation of Non-ulcer Dyspepsia by Gastric Biopsy," *Br Med J* 1 (1957): 372-77.

6. H. Moldofsky, et al., "Musculoskeletal Symptoms and Non-REM Sleep Disturbance in Patients with 'Fibrositis' Syndrome and Healthy Subjects," *Psychosom Med* 37 (1975): 341-51.

7. R. J. Arthur, "Life Stress and Disease: An Appraisal of the Concept," in *Critical Issues in Behavioral Medicine,* ed. L. J. West and M. Stein (Philadelphia: J. B. Lippincott, 1982), 3-17.

CHAPTER *3*

Exhaustion: A Short Fuse

Tired. *That's all he could think about as he moved in slow motion through his day, which began with a 5:30 A.M. hospital visit. From breakfast appointment to staff meeting to phone calls to a thousand interruptions, he tried to act responsible, creative, sensitive, and awake. By lunchtime, he was really dragging and used several cups of coffee to create some much-needed artificial energy. The schedule didn't let up in the evening. Every night there had been something, and tonight it was discipleship training. On and on, his calendar demands arched as a monster devouring every bit of energy and free time that should have been his. As days of this unpredictable and pounding schedule continued, he found it harder and harder to cover the weight of fatigue he felt. Even weekends provided little relief because of home and family responsibilities. He dreaded another day, another appointment, another meeting. If he could just push through this blur. If he could just get some rest. But it was a luxury his schedule would not permit.*

Exhaustion. How many relationships has it affected? How many perspectives skewed? How many times has it dented or destroyed a person's commitment to ministry and call?

Exhaustion lurks as a major contributor to disease, ill health, and accidents. Sleep-deprived workers on rotating graveyard shifts experience more illness, more accidents, and more absence. Medically speaking, exhaustion presents symptoms from inability to stay awake for routine tasks to palpitations of the heart, high blood pressure, and other occurrences that could point to a serious physical problem. Exhaustion affects perspective, problem-solving skills, interpersonal relationships, motivation, endurance, and the immune system.

Exhausted to Begin With

Many Christian leaders begin ministry tasks already tired from a busy life. Is it any wonder that they find ministry draining, unfulfilling, and without joy? And who is to blame? The church and all the uncommitted people? Our society and all the unrealistic expectations? Our God and a call that establishes no boundaries? Who gets the blame?

It is my experience that Christians tend to blame their weariness on external circumstances: other people, society, or their ministry. For example, too many interruptions make it necessary to work late consistently. Too many noes from uncommitted parishioners push pastors to overextend themselves. It's easy to fill in the blanks of if-only statements with names and events. However, the Bible reveals that a weary, burned-out, unfocused, disillusioned life results from being outside of God's will, not in it!

The Bible reveals that a weary, burned-out, unfocused, disillusioned life results from being outside of God's will, not in it!

Indeed, God calls His children to take on tasks that require investing substantial emotional and physical energy. It is also true that the human body has inherent human limitations. Both of these facts mean that every Christian will experience episodes of tiredness. It is inevitable. However, the Bible does not use an exhausted lifestyle as a model for committed ministry.

Consider the following foundational characteristics from various scriptures that draw a picture of a Spirit-filled Christian.

Gal. 5:22-23	*Phil. 4:7-11*	*Acts 1:8*
Love, joy, peace	Peace, truth	power
patience	honorable, right	
kindness	pure, lovely	
goodness	good reputation	
faithfulness	excellent	
gentleness	praiseworthy	
self-control		

Nowhere does it list exhaustion. Instead, the one who is in the center of God's will is a man or woman of resolve, strength, focus, joy, purity, and power! Exhaustion only blurs these characteristics.

Make no mistake, human beings do not innately possess these qualities, nor can they develop them on their own. Paul voices this struggle when he states that innate goodness does not come from being human (Rom. 7:18). The physical body is not invincible. It is weak. It has limits. Sometimes those limits overpower good intentions, as the disciples found out when they could not keep their eyes open to pray for their Master (Matt. 26:40-43). In fact, when we come to God, we bring the weary and weak part of our humanity. When God plants himself in us through His Holy Spirit, He gives us the strong and powerful part of His character (Gal. 2:20). It is that transformation that makes the difference.

Perhaps the question many ask is, *How much difference does Christ's strength make?* After all, we know that our bodies are limited and the work of ministry is unending. Isn't it unreasonable to expect anything but a life of tired, methodical obedience without the hope of real rest until Christ gives us a resurrected body? Paul answered this question with a resounding no! Second Cor. 12:9-10 reminds us that God's power works mightily in human weakness. The result of this weakness-made-strong is a life marked by victory and abundance, not fatigue and exhaustion.

How Goes the Battle?

I will never forget the time, as a high school boy, when I heard my youth pastor talk of attending ministerial meetings. He described, sadly, that the most frequent question at such gatherings was "How goes the battle?" He would then watch many of his ordained colleagues live and labor for years under circumstances that never became any more than one continuous life of exhausting labor, filled with too many failures and too few victories. This simply is not consistent with the biblical description of Christian life and ministry.

Have times changed that much since the days of the New Testament Church? Today governmental intervention, church boards, complaining parishioners, and a culture that is depraved beyond belief offer challenges that New Testament Church leaders never faced. It is easy to think that the Early Church leaders did not have to deal with complex problems, that life was much simpler. But look at their *simple* problems. Stoning, crucifixion, imprisonment, beatings, and other *noncomplex* issues. How could anyone come to believe that today's ministry is much harder than it was for our predecessors?

When Ministry Was REALLY Tough

The apostle Paul gave one of the clearest examples of what the empowering Holy Spirit can do to bring joy, peace, and victory despite enormous adversity. In 2 Cor. 11:23-27 he expressed it this way:

> [I suffered] imprisonments, [was] beaten times without number, often in danger of death. Five times I received from the Jews thirty-nine lashes. Three times I was beaten with rods, once I was stoned, three times I was shipwrecked, a night and a day I have spent in the deep. I have been on frequent journeys, in dangers from rivers, dangers from robbers, dangers from my countrymen, dangers from the Gentiles, dangers in the city, dangers in the wilderness, dangers on the sea, dangers among false brethren; I have been in labor and hardship, through many sleepless nights, in hunger and thirst, often without food, in cold and exposure.

After this litany of pressures, threats, and dangers, one would expect the next verse to be an exhausted complaint if not an admission of full-blown burnout. But the words take an astonishing twist, and verse 28 reveals the power and focus that Paul experienced when he says, "Apart from such *external* things, there is the daily pressure upon me of concern for all the churches" (emphasis added). Imagine a man experiencing this list of catastrophes in verses 23-27 and then characterizing them as merely "external things"! They appear almost trivial to Paul. But that's not all. Not only does he seem to downplay his hardships, but also he finishes with the affirmation that his primary daily interest is his "concern for all the churches." What an incredible testimony to remain so focused on the church while suffering so many blows.

Is modern ministry more difficult than what Paul faced? In many ways it is much easier. However, modern ministry faces a more destructive temptation that is to blame for its exhausted servants. It is possible to achieve certain kinds of success simply by relying on human strength and ability and to equate success with carrying out God's plan.

Second Cor. 11 exposes this wrong conclusion and gives great encouragement. Paul emphasizes what God can do through committed Christian leaders, no matter the circumstances. The only requirement is complete surrender to His perfect will. This allows the Spirit's empowerment (4:16-18; 5:7). Indeed, we don't need an easier or less complex ministry. Rather, we need Christian leaders who will focus on one thing: to "know Him, and the power of His resurrection" (Phil. 3:10). No matter how difficult the day feels, He calls His servants for such a time as this. He calls them not to exhaustion but to power and strength.

> **Why are so many ministers too tired to experience this weakness-to-strength empowerment?**

Then, why are so many ministers too tired to experience this weakness-to-strength empowerment? Why does exhaustion seem to consume the best part of God's servants? Does God expect too much in today's complicated world? Does the church expect too much?

I would suggest that the major cause of weariness and exhaustion in today's ministers is not a church problem, an organizational problem, or even a commitment problem. Simply stated, we are too busy. It's not God's fault. It's not the church's fault. It's our fault.

Tired Saints

Ministers aren't the only ones experiencing the problem of exhaustion. And that's part of the ministry problem. Everyone is exhausted. The church people bring minds and bodies that are exhausted from busy lives. When these people add ministries to their already frantic lifestyles, a puzzling turn of events occurs. What began as a way to serve the Lord degenerates into an opportunity to blame the church for asking too much. Overcommitment exposes their sense of weariness, disillusionment, and even anger. Suddenly, the church is at fault.

I have seen many people who fill nearly every waking hour with secular activities when they should have been spending some of those hours asleep. If asked to give one or two hours a week to the church, they blame their exhaustion on their ministry responsibilities, not the other activities. Some even have time for many hours of TV, but not a couple of hours preparing for a Sunday School lesson. In other words, the straw blamed for breaking the camel's back is less than 1 percent of the gross weight of the camel.

It's the same trap that ministers face: blaming external circumstances for personal choices. The pastors of tired people must find a way to help them understand that their busyness is not the church's fault! *But pastors cannot teach what they do not model!* First, ministers must face the issue of personal choice. They must understand that the path of obedience requires prioritizing their *too busy* list according to God's approval. This must include all issues, not just ministry ones. Balance is the key. Not only balance between secular activity and ministry but also balance between rest and any activity.

As a whole, Christians need to do more ministry and far less of everything else. However, the person whose life contains too much work and stress does not find the answer by adding ministry activities. The answer is learning how to identify and balance priorities.

When many of your people are as exhausted as you are for much the same reason, the leader must realize that the problem is more than a matter of commitment. If only a handful of laypeople take care of the majority of ministry positions within the local church, it is easy to take advantage of their willingness and praise such *commitment*. However, is overcommitment that leads to exhaustion the kind of commitment God honors? In situations like this, both the shepherd and the sheep contribute to the problem of exhaustion. This results in compromising God's plan for building His Church.

When was the last time that you identified a ministry need but refused to ask anyone to meet it until you had asked the Lord whom He desired in that ministry role? When was the last time you allowed a vacancy to remain while you waited for God's answer, no matter how long it took? There is no substitute for waiting on God before filling ministry positions. Any other method will always get in the way of God's perfect plan. Be silent. Wait. Listen. Let God arrange the parts of the Body (1 Cor. 12:18).

Intense Ministry—Peaceful Heart

In 2 Cor. 11:23-28 we identified Paul's time-consuming and energy-draining ministry. However, he was able to maintain unshakable stamina and zeal for several reasons. First, he understood that it is Christ who will save the world and build the Church (Matt. 16:18). Second, he was willing to appropriate God's power in his life and did not depend upon his own strength to accomplish his ministry (2 Cor. 12:9-10). Third, while his life was one of committed ministry activity, it was also one of prayer and rest (Phil. 4:6-7).

No man could have done what Paul did by human strength. The truth is that God has called every one of us to a ministry that is far beyond our ability and strength. This ministry simply cannot be accomplished apart from heavenly power. Given Paul's intense ministry, it is hard to understand how he seemed so tireless. It was because he followed God's will in every aspect of his life, including taking care of his earthen vessel. He didn't just give his exhaustion to God. He submitted the choices that could have led to emotional and physical exhaustion. We must do the same if we are to fulfill God's call for our lives.

Burnout in the Modern Church

Burnout is a modern Christian problem. It was not even discussed in New Testament writings. Yes, there were times of suffering and pain and weariness and sorrow. But there was no pattern of intense ministry followed by physical, emotional, and mental exhaustion. No one testified to being *too tired* to continue service to the Kingdom. In fact, the apostle John was over 80 when he wrote five books of the New Testament between A.D. 95 and 100.

We have followed a frantic culture into a frenzied life and blame God for it.

Why is it such a problem today? Perhaps because we have followed a frantic culture into a frenzied life and blame God for it. We have allowed long work hours, late night mindlessness in front of television sets, and nonstop activities to claim our time, our focus, our joy, our health, our peace, and our hearts. Perhaps the greatest tragedy is that Jesus stands, waiting for us to come and dine with Him, to receive promised rest and strength. But Jesus will not eat on the run! Fast food is not His way! He desires to control every part of our lives. He will be Lord of all or not Lord at all. Isn't that the message preached from the pulpits of our churches? Is a ministry servant exempt from making this same application to daily choices that threaten to compromise the leader's ability to achieve balance between work and rest?

The Far-reaching Effects

The problem of exhaustion is not simply a problem that affects a minister's individual life. It has devastating effects on God's plan to save the world. Like the disciples who failed in Gethsemane, we have been working when we should have been resting, and sleeping when we should have been praying.

Like them, when it is time to be alert and ready to minister, we find ourselves exhausted to the point of collapse.

How many times has the ministry of the church been compromised because the children of God were just too tired? Indeed, the mighty army of God strikes terror in the mind of the enemy when it is moving forward in God's strength. However, it is no army at all when the soldiers can't stay awake for the battle.

No Burnout in This Guy

A great example of one who was prepared to answer the call of God, even in his old age, was the prophet Haggai. After the Exile, a small remnant of the Jews returned to build the Temple at Jerusalem under the leadership of Zerubbabel. Soon after starting, they confronted adversaries who discouraged and frightened them so much that the rebuilding ceased (Ezra 4:4-5).

At this time, the elderly prophet Haggai, despite his age and the discouraging spiritual times in Judah, was ready to answer the call of God. Haggai encouraged Ezra, Zechariah, and the sons of Judah to lead the Jews to begin the rebuilding once again. It was through the encouraging prophecy of an old man that God was able to accomplish His great plan. Clearly, Haggai had spent his life spiritually, mentally, and physically prepared for God's call. Not everyone was dejected, exhausted, forlorn, and depressed. Haggai was awake and listening when the call came (Ezra 5:1-2).

How many "temples" could we rebuild if God's children were not too tired to answer His call? The life of this great prophet should challenge each of us to ask whether we are obeying God by being rested as well as ready.

As you examine yourself, do you find weariness that you have blamed on the church or people or ministry or God? I don't mean a "good tired" that comes after working hard for God's kingdom while experiencing and seeing His perfect will accomplished. I'm talking about weariness with resentment, weariness with anger, weariness without hope of resolution.

The Yoke That Fits

We must examine this weariness carefully. It may not be the church's fault. It may be that we wear the wrong yoke (Matt. 11:29-30). We have accepted one that doesn't fit right. We have forgotten that it is a double-collared yoke and have failed to share the burden with Jesus. Jesus himself promised that when we take His yoke, the burden is easy and light. It fits just right! This truth from chapter 11 isn't new information to you. What pastor has not preached with passion from this passage? However, there is a truth within this passage that few have noticed.

Prior to the "yoke" paragraph, Jesus was discussing how unwise that generation had been. They had rejected the message of John the Baptist just as previous generations had rejected the Law and the Prophets (v. 13). Then, in verses 21-23, He names and rebukes the cities that had not repented: the cities of Chorazin, Bethsaida, and Capernaum.

Then comes the paragraph that we have been reviewing in verses 25-30. Isn't this an odd place for Jesus to deal with the issue of yoke wearing and rest? What in the world do these words have to do with His previous statements?

In verse 25 Jesus begins: "I praise you, Father, Lord of heaven and earth, because you have hidden these things from the wise and learned, and revealed them to little children" (NIV). He then goes on to make an amazing statement in verse 27: "All things have been committed to me by my Father. No one knows the Son except the Father, and no one knows the Father except the Son *and those to whom the Son chooses to reveal him*" (NIV, emphasis added). What a revealing statement! No one will ever come to know the Father except those to whom Christ wills to reveal Him.

To Whom Will Jesus Reveal the Father?

Here's the key concept! Let us never forget the link to His next statement. The next three verses promise rest and light burdens for those to whom Jesus reveals the Father. It is at this exact point that Jesus says, "Come to me, all you who are weary and burdened, and I will give you rest. Take my yoke upon you and learn from me, for I am gentle and humble in heart, and you will find rest for your souls. For my yoke is easy and my burden is light" (vv. 28-30, NIV). To whom will Jesus reveal His Father? To the one who wears the yoke that Christ gives him or her! And from whom will the true knowledge of the Father be withheld? From the one who wears *any other yoke*, no matter how successful it has made that person!

Without meaning to, some of my pastor friends tell me which yoke they wear. Some wear the needy people yoke and make all decisions based on other people's needs. Some wear a church board yoke because they feel collared to please them. Some wear a church hierarchy yoke, feeling caught between the demands of loyalty and leadership. This leads to a terrifying question: *Does the very nature of modern ministry place pastors in a position where they are least likely to know the heart of God?* The thought is almost overwhelming. On the one hand, modern ministry calls one to work and labor. But Jesus has already said that the ones to whom He reveals His Father, He calls to rest, to an easy yoke and a light load.

The symptoms of this problem and a hint of its magnitude appeared in a recent survey of over 1,000 senior pastors. It showed that "four out of ten pastors doubt that their present church experience is significantly deepening their relationship with Christ."[1] This is a staggering statistic. Almost half of those surveyed find themselves in an assignment unattached to the yoke that promises to reveal deeper lessons about the Father.

There is no doubt that modern ministry is a heavy load. There are days when there is no other way to complete all the

> To whom will Jesus reveal His Father? To the one who wears the yoke that Christ gives him or her! And from whom will the true knowledge of the Father be withheld? From the one who wears *any other yoke*, no matter how successful it has made that person!

activities except to come home tired with just enough energy to fall into bed. But is that the lifestyle God intended to accompany His call?

Exhaustion is part of the time bomb contributing to burnout and a host of other problems for the modern minister.

Exhaustion is the short fuse that speeds up some form of eruption. But what lights the fuse? What motivations, choices, or situations strike the spark that initiates the quick burn to explosion? Keep reading. After a good night's sleep, that is.

WHAT ABOUT YOU?

- Do you blame the church for your busy schedule?
- Do you try to fill too many vacancies by overextending yourself?
- Do you know how to balance rest and activity?
- Have you cultivated a peaceful heart in the middle of intense ministry?
- Do you wear the right yoke?

ENDNOTES

1. George Barna, *Today's Pastors* (Ventura, Calif.: Regal Books, 1993), 59.

CHAPTER 4

Who Lit the Fuse?

If exhaustion is a short fuse that leads to explosions contributing to burnout, then who or what lights the fuse? Is it a physical problem? Is it a personality flaw? Do pastors just work too hard? Are they too committed? Unfortunately, it takes more than getting extra sleep to combat the problem. It takes honest introspection while entreating the Holy Spirit to be the uncompromising Guide into truth.

However, before I could write one word to pastors about this subject, the Holy Spirit had to speak volumes to me. You see, the same tendencies and commitment issues tempt me to rationalize and condone overwork. Emergency medicine can be a lot like pastoral ministry. Like you, my work is never done. Someone always needs my services. Many of the needs are critical to the point of life and death. What right do I have to enjoy my family when someone is dying? Just like you, I can make a case for being on call 24 hours a day. Like you, I can push my physical boundaries to the point of exhaustion. However, what good is it to save one life and be unavailable for 75 others the next day? That is why I speak with such passion. I am speaking for the hundreds of people in the days to come who need you just as much. Also, I want to make sure that your family finds their priority place for critical care as you try to provide many kinds of administrative and emergency service for others.

The first step in addressing the exhaustion problem is to stop blaming other people's problems for our crisis. Instead, focus on what is *within* our control. Look beyond schedule and expectations, needs and responsibilities. What ultimately pushes anyone to exhaustion? Choices. But what motivates those choices? There's where we will find specific ways to combat the problem. It will require a deep look into the mirror of your very being. Are you ready to take that look?

A Matter of Choice

How many times do your words or actions say the following: *I don't have time to do something with the family. I don't have time for leisure. I don't have time for myself.* And why not? Because you have to fulfill a ministry responsibility. Obviously, there are always times in any job when work responsibilities identify a priority and preclude any other activity. However, there is a problem when it becomes the routine instead of the exception.

Why do we make such choices? Why can't we leave ministry responsibilities at regular intervals? Why can't we leave them in God's hands? Why do we create such imbalance that harms one group of people to help another?

The Danger of Self-sufficiency

While there are many reasons, there is one that surfaces as a culprit more than others. Don't reject it without careful examination. It is a form of self-sufficiency with overtones of insecurity that subtly suggests that unless you can do it all, you aren't fulfilling the Great Commission. It is that inside voice that, quite frankly, you have confused to be God's voice. It says you've got to do more, do it better, do it bigger, and do it for more people. Stated most simply, it's pride. Pride places confidence in your own skills. Right away, you can see the tightrope. You have to use your God-given skills. That's why He gave them to you. However, you can't depend on them. Dependence pushes you to accept responsibility you were never made to carry: the responsibility for success, including the success of the gospel. Those who live this way show that they do not believe God is capable of carrying out His plan to save the world. No amount of mental, verbal, or theological homage to God releases people from the responsibility to honor His sovereignty.

Pride is the greatest of all indulgences. In fact, many theologians believe that the opposite of righteousness is not sinfulness but pride, the essence of self-will. Consequently, specific sins are symptoms of the fundamental problem of pride. The foundations of the struggle (and chasm) between God and humanity are problems of will and evidenced in acts of sin. The most basic issue is that of lordship. Either I submit to all of the implications of His sovereignty, or I live in the self-deception that I am my own lord. In this area, as in others, partial obedience is disobedience.

Saul's Example

King Saul was a tragic example of this problem. In the 15th chapter of 1 Samuel, God spoke through Samuel to tell Saul to attack the Amalekites and completely destroy every person and possession. Initially, Saul obeyed. However, when the battle dust settled, Saul made some exceptions to God's instructions and spared the king and the best of his livestock (v. 9). In other words, Saul obeyed only that portion of God's command that he was willing to obey.

When the prophet Samuel discovered what Saul and the people had done, he confronted Saul with his sin. Saul's response revealed his pride: "I *did* obey the voice of the LORD" (v. 20, emphasis added). Unfortunately, Saul found out too late that the consequence for partial obedience is severe. God's judgment was clear in the words of the prophet: "Because you have rejected the word of the LORD, He has also rejected you from being king" (v. 23).

A Clear Message

The message of this story should be clear: Partial obedience is disobedience! Choosing to obey His call to serve but not His call to rest, balance, and submission compromises His plan for the ministry to which He calls His servants. Living like this reveals an underlying sense of self-sufficiency, indeed pride.

This issue of partial obedience is easy to identify in others' lives. When you look at parishioners' lives and see them obeying God's call to rest but not His call to ministry, what do you call it? Sin! Now let's ask God what He would call it when His minister obeys His call to service but not His call to sabbath. We're doing what Saul did. We're obeying only the commands that we choose to.

The Myth of Self-help

Currently, the popular concept that humanity has unlimited potential sweeps the country with self-help programs to encourage developing a positive self-image and the power of positive thinking. However, any philosophy that believes that we can do anything that we set our minds to or that we can improve ourselves using the "good that is within us" is pure, unadulterated humanism. After all, what is humanism but the idolatry of humanity?

The human potential movement represents pride in its most advanced and misleading form.

The human potential movement represents pride in its most advanced and misleading form. Solving humanity's problems by humankind's own potential is impossible because sinful people will never have the answers for a sinful world. After many millennia of humanity attempting to solve the problems of the world by human intelligence, the world is no closer to the truth than it has ever been. Once again we are in another "New Age" that promises peace, prosperity, health, wealth, and the end of poverty. Unfortunately, the problems are far too complex for humans to fix. Despite this fact, various philosophers, historians, and world leaders continue to argue with each other about the best way to create another Great Society. In their blindness, humanity fails to recognize that we are much like the two flies on a horse's back who are arguing about which one of them owns the animal.

The Messiah Complex

To add to the erroneous beliefs generated by the human potential movement, many church leaders and pastors suffer from a "messiah complex." Christian leaders have been very good at identifying false prophets and "saviors" who proclaimed themselves "messiah" (e.g., Joseph Smith, David Koresh, Sun Myung Moon, Jim Jones, etc.). However, they have not been as good at identifying *within themselves* a similar tendency to view their ministry as absolutely essential to the salvation of those around them. Although they certainly shun the apostasy associated with false messiahs, they seem to miss the similarities. Their lifestyle betrays an underlying sense that the Kingdom will not advance without their overwork. Thus, they labor on, day after day, month after month, year after year, tired, weary, depressed, and sometimes disillusioned.

What God Can Do in My Absence

Many church leaders fail to recognize that God actually *wants* them to leave ministry tasks *routinely*. However, the enhancement of their spiritual, mental, and physical health is not the only reason. God wants to do His sovereign work during their absence.

> **God works in our absence in ways that He cannot in our presence!**

God works in our absence in ways that He cannot in our presence! In other words, God wants us out of the way so that He can accomplish things that He will not do if we are present. In fact, sometimes when we are working the hardest, we may actually be compromising His plan by simply hanging on too tightly. This leads to a fundamental question that cannot go unanswered: *Do we really believe that God can carry out His will?* "Of course He can," we quickly emphasize as we continue our frantic push to do His work. It's just that He can't accomplish His purpose without me!

What can God do without us? Well, He can use someone else. God desires to use other people in our absence that He cannot use if we are always available! God calls people to ministries during the absence of others because an apparent need is an exposed need. Exposed needs are terrifying to many pastors. I have seen pastors prevent an announcement about vacancies in children's ministries because they feared it presented a weak picture to visiting families. But who made the pastors responsible for what others won't do? They seem to have missed an important point. Often, God uses an exposed need to call people to service and ministry. Keeping needs covered by filling holes too quickly may prevent God's call in the lives of your people.

There is another important way that God works during the absence of Christian leaders. No matter how successful a ministry is, *no one* brings only strengths to the work. Everyone has weaknesses, areas of blindness, personality quirks, idiosyncrasies, and a substantial dose of humanity.

Just think about taking yourself out of your ministry picture for a day, a week, or more, and what's the first thing that comes to your mind? *How will they make it?* We understand that when we are not filling our ministry slot, the church must survive without the strengths God has provided to accomplish the task. It's easy to think that we cheat the church out of something that God wants them to have. However, let's be totally honest with ourselves and reject the myths that pride would have us believe. At the same time the ministry *misses* our strengths, it enjoys a reprieve from our weaknesses!

Part of God's plan for frequently cycling us out of our ministries is so that He can use other people's strengths. It would be a sad commentary on us if we prevent God from doing all that He desires to do in our ministry simply because we are never willing to get out of the way.

My Story

Recently the Lord revealed this to me in a very personal way. In our local church I teach an adult Sunday School class. We have an accountability list of approximately 100 and average approximately 60 in attendance. I believe that the Lord has used this class to help move His kingdom forward in a small but significant way in our local congregation. I take my teaching responsibilities very seriously.

Because my education is in medicine and not theology, it has taken me countless hours to prepare for this class over the past 12 years. Part of my commitment has been to limit the number of Sundays that I am gone. However, due to clinical responsibilities and medical conferences, sometimes I have to miss the class.

Not too long ago, I recruited our pastor's wife to teach the class on a Sunday that I had to be away. She is a gifted teacher with a deep knowledge of God's Word. I asked her to take the class because I knew that she would take the commitment seriously and prepare effectively.

On my return, one of my class members told me that she had done an outstanding job. I was pleased to hear this good report. It was exactly what I had hoped for. However, his next statement caught me unprepared. He said, "If you get her to be the substitute, you can feel free to leave town anytime." In that statement, God showed me that there are many things that He wants to do in the lives of the people around me that He can only accomplish when I leave my responsibilities behind. God was working in my absence in ways that He could not have in my presence.

Just Take Away the Pain

In my practice of emergency medicine, I frequently care for patients who are suffering from acute, severe abdominal pain. Often, the patient's first concern is relief from pain. Frequently, patients and their family pressure me to give pain medication early in the course of evaluation. From their perspective, this serves a very important purpose: decrease pain; decrease suffering. What better treatment exists? They believe it must be good for them because it makes them happier and more comfortable. It also makes them view me as a thoughtful, caring, compassionate physician. However, if I grant their wishes, I have done the worst possible thing for them. This is true because many of the life-threatening causes for acute abdominal pain are only revealed when a physician can monitor the signs and symptoms of the problem as they unfold over time. As the attending physician, I must allow the problem to expose itself or risk further complications to the patient's condition. In a paradoxical way, allowing the patient to suffer is the best thing for him or her. This is why I am willing to face substantial pressure and often animosity from the patient and family. I have committed to identify and treat the real problem. Here's the tough part: to be a *good* physician, I have to be willing for some to call me a *bad* physician.

In the Body of Christ, as with the human body, it is easier to relieve symptoms instead of solving core issues.

In the Body of Christ, as with the human body, it is easier to relieve symptoms instead of solving core issues. However, we are not interested in merely relieving symptoms. For example, a pastor can recruit some children's Sunday School teachers to fill some holes; but if he or she does not address the real issue, whether it is organization or leadership, the problem will occur again, usually somewhere else. The same is true for people dealing with family issues, marriage issues, and sin issues. We desire for people and the church body to be cured! Although exposed needs within the body may overwhelm the leader, they are a tool in God's sovereign hand. Here's the tough part: to be a good pastor, you have to be willing for some to think you are a bad pastor.

Chosen for Weakness

It is true that God tends to place people in ministry based upon their gifts and strengths. In fact, this is one of the paradigms of the church growth discipline. However, it is not the rule. Scripture reveals that sometimes God chooses people because of their weaknesses. He does this to remind us that, unless we surrender to His sovereignty and understand our total dependence upon Him, we are living by some measure of self-effort that the Bible calls pride.

The Creator has a long history of choosing inadequate people to do great things for Him. Jeremiah and Timothy were too young (Jer. 1:4-10; 1 Tim. 4:12). Ruth had the wrong ancestry (Ruth 1:4). Paul was physically unimpressive (2 Cor. 10:10). Amos had the wrong education and profession (Amos 1:1). David was too small (1 Sam. 16:6-13). Peter and John were uneducated (Acts 4:13-14).

Moses: the Wrong Man for the Job?

When God called Moses, He called a man of many weaknesses. He was an unknown desert shepherd. He had no authority except over his herds. He no longer had any credibility in Pharaoh's Egypt. And worst of all, he lacked confidence in his speaking ability.

God responded to each of Moses' weaknesses with His strength. To the problem of identity, God gave him His identity (Exod. 3:9-12). To the problem of credibility, God showed him how He would transform simple things into the miraculous (4:2-9). To the problem of eloquence, God reminded him that the One who created his mouth could supply the words (vv. 11-12). What an awesome message. For each inadequacy that Moses confessed, God had an answer and a plan.

God didn't just choose Moses as a man of strength. He chose him as a man with inadequacies as well. Why? Because Moses had to surrender his sense of adequacy so that God could accomplish the impossible through him. To go to Pharaoh with any attitude of self-sufficiency would have been a death wish.

Moses' call from God shows us how He desires to use every aspect of our lives. In a way that only He could conceive, He may be more interested in our limitations than in our strengths. Never forget that even in our finest moments, at the peak of our talents, we are powerless prey before the forces of darkness. But that is the beauty of God's plan to save the world. He doesn't depend on our strength but on our submission. Paul articulates how our Creator uses our inadequacies to carry out His will in 2 Cor. 12:9-10 by announcing His prescription for weakness: "'My grace is sufficient for you, for power is perfected in weakness.' Most gladly, therefore, I will rather boast about my weaknesses, that the power of Christ may dwell in me. Therefore I am well content with weaknesses . . . for Christ's sake; for when I am weak, then I am strong."

Jesus Chose a Motley Crew

Little needs to be said about the weaknesses, quirks, and mediocre skills of the Twelve. When I think about it, I am amazed that Jesus asked ordinary people to join Him in His ministry. Nevertheless, Jesus chose these Twelve in spite of the fact that they were less skilled, less wise, and less committed. This did not keep Him from involving them in ministry. Neither did it keep Him from leaving them in places of ministry when He went to the wilderness to pray at times during His ministry. Even more astonishing is the fact that Christ ultimately left His future plans for saving the world in the hands of inherently inadequate people.

The Mystery of the Church

It is hard to believe that Jesus left His plan for saving humankind in the hands of humans, even if they were Spirit-filled. Isn't this the same discomfort that church leaders experience when they delegate ministry to "less gifted" individuals? But this hesitation becomes absurd when you think of this: Jesus turned His earthly ministry over to us! So why do we cling to our ministry tasks when the perfect, all-powerful Son of God modeled handing His work to far less capable hands than His own?

We Thought We Could Do Anything

During the 1940s and 1950s, Evangelicalism enjoyed great successes in this country. The institutional church grew to unprecedented size and impacted society more intensely than ever before. Evangelical Christianity successfully accomplished everything it attempted.

Add to this the profound cultural impact of the World War II victory, especially as a victory of good over evil. This left our society with a great sense of invincibility. Economic success pervaded this unprecedented time. In addition to all of this, a generation of scientists made the impossible look like child's play. In the midst of these achievements, a fundamental change occurred in the attitude of Christian leaders with regard to their ability to win spiritual victories. This change was subtle, deceptive, and almost unnoticed. We lost the awareness of our total weakness apart from absolute reliance on the empowering Holy Spirit! As this change occurred, many pastors began to work in their own strength and by their own plans. They stopped inquiring of the Lord. They stopped seeking His plans. They stopped searching for how God desired to fight the battles. This was a tragic setup for today's generation of pastors.

Today, the nature of the church and of our society has changed greatly. While we have a healthy awareness of the battle stakes and clearly understand we cannot win in our own strength, we still miss the message of weakness made strong. We are a church on the run. We watch an epidemic of church splits and an enormous attrition of broken, defeated pastors. But this is not surprising. The failure of God's appointed leaders to remain absolutely dependent upon His strength has always had devastating consequences.

The Failure at Ai

The Ai failure was a dramatic point in the history of Israel. Under Joshua's leadership, the nation had experienced an overwhelming victory over the mightily fortified Jericho. Riding high on the wave of this victory, they felt invincible. They won the victory by marching around a great city, blowing trumpets. How much easier could it get? Evidently, it never crossed their minds that the little town of Ai could possibly resist the power they proved at Jericho. So they took only a small force of soldiers and demonstrated the vulnerability pride inflicts.

Tragically, Joshua did not fully recognize that it had been God's power and not his military prowess that won the battle. Because of this, he did not ask God how to attack Ai or whether they were to engage in the battle at all. This presumption left out God's leadership and power and led to a miserable defeat and the death of 36 Israelites.

We still fight our Ais. We push ahead with assumption rather than God's direction. We fall prey to self-sufficiency instead of accessing God's all-power. If there is any hope for true revival, every spiritual leader must confess weakness and accept God's antidotal strength.

New Understandings

Have you seen yourself in these pages? Are you a pastor who has substituted overwork for obedience to God? Have you limited God's ability to move freely among His people because you are so busy with your agenda? Physical and emotional exhaustion tinged with overtones of failure waits for anyone who attempts to build the church by his or her own strength. Allowing God to use our strengths and relying on our strengths is the difference between submission and self-rule. What the church needs most are pastors who are aware of their fragility, weakness, and absolute inability to do anything of eternal significance in their own power. What your people need most is a pastor who knows how to "cease striving" (Ps. 46:10)! They need you to ask yourself if you are an accomplice to the time bomb in the church!

Physical and emotional exhaustion . . . waits for anyone who attempts to build the church by his or her own strength.

Could it be that the church is only effective when her leaders understand how to identify and submit any raw edge of pride? Our problem is not the strength of the enemy. God has never cowered before the powers of darkness. He is not the least bit concerned that they will ever catch Him by surprise. In His all-knowledge, He knows every intricate detail of each spiritual battle that will occur. Before the foundations of the earth, He knew every problem that we would ever face.

We can no longer blame our defeats only on the great strength of Satan's forces! Jesus has already seen Satan fall (Luke 10:18). Again I say, our problem is not the strength of the enemy. Our problem is our failure to rely completely on the Father.

The Answer

The answer to the ticking time bomb is not better plans, even though prudent plans are important. The answer is not more strengths, although God certainly gifts each servant with important tools of the trade. The answer lies in pleasing God. Clearly He has told us over and over that pride and any of its relatives of self-sufficiency or arrogance always displeases Him. He asks us to address the motives for overwork and imbalance. He instructs us to stop blaming anyone or anything but our own choices for the schedules that push us to overwork and exhaustion. He invites us to prove His miracle of weakness made strong. Living His answer brings much more victory than anything a crowded schedule could produce!

There is also a much more basic answer to the internal and external stresses that go with the life of ministry. Again, the answer comes from God. It is almost too simple. However, that doesn't mean it is easy to obey, as we'll discover in the next chapter.

WHAT ABOUT YOU?

- **Do small battles appear impossible and leave you exhausted?**
- **Do you find yourself retreating from problems?**
- **Do you confuse relying on your strengths with submitting them to God?**

- Do you allow God to make the plans you are to carry out?

- Do you revert to a form of self-sufficiency to get the work done?

- Do you work to relieve symptoms of exhaustion without addressing your overcrowded schedule?

- Are you willing to let God use your weaknesses to bring about strength?

CHAPTER 5

God's Prescription

While the time bomb ticks, good pastors with sincere calls, effective experience, and committed hearts continue to follow patterns that place them in the pathway of an explosion. They rely on the need for adrenaline to produce energy for their stressed schedules. They fall prey to a ministry-produced numbing, which makes them unaware of the physical damage stress causes. They blame the wrong causes for overwork and busy schedules. They do not connect health issues with any of these factors. They become casualties of a physical or emotional time bomb that has the potential to create unnecessary detours in their journey to answer God's call in their lives.

But God calls servants to ministry, not to burnout. Then how can ministers protect themselves from a time bomb they do not hear ticking?

Does it surprise you that God has a prescription? It prevents unnecessary problems and protects health and ministry. It's very simple to understand and very difficult to apply. To understand the plan, we have to look at the time when God set His plan in motion. We have to go back to one of the busiest and most productive times of the ages. We have to go back to the beginning.

In the Beginning

Genesis tells us that after God created, He rested. He modeled the principle of resting after productive activity before the day had a name. By the time of Moses, the Hebrew word *shabbat* was used to name the seventh day. It simply meant *to cease, to desist*. Long after creation, the Ten Commandments repeated it as the fourth law. God clearly outlined it again in the precept of sabbatical rest in Mosaic Law (Lev. 25:1-7).

To understand this principle, we must return to the fundamental, God-ordained concept of the Sabbath rest that involves more than a day, more than rules, and more than worship. It involves a cycle, a rhythm, a pattern. It involves a fundamental principle of obedience that influences lifestyle priorities. The implications of the sabbatical principle continue to impact our lives today.

> **The Sabbath rest . . . involves a cycle, a rhythm, a pattern . . . a fundamental principle of obedience.**

The Sabbath Cycle

God initiated a cycle based on seven. The number seven and its multiples occur in many places in the Bible. One of the most revealing places involves the seven-year cycle as applied to the land.

For six years, God's people toiled on the land. However, during the seventh year, those who tilled the soil were to cease their work for a year. To a nation that depended on agriculture for its existence, this must have been a very puzzling and frightening command. How could they afford to stop harvesting every seventh year? It would compromise their survival. It simply made no sense! So God's people did not obey.

Good Reasons to Disobey

There is little doubt that many of those who disobeyed the sabbatical law had excellent reasons for doing so. After all, God had blessed their six years with prosperous harvests. Didn't it make sense that if they continued working the land during the seventh year, there would be more resources to carry out His plans? They wanted to fulfill their covenant relationship with God. Certainly, working hard and rejecting a year off would show Him how serious they were. On and on they justified disobedience.

Unfortunately, the Israelites did not understand that disobedience would actually *compromise* God's plan for His nation and would *limit* the resources available for His plans. They did not understand the purpose for the sabbatical cycle.

The purpose of the sabbatical year was to allow the land to rest so that in the long run it would bear more bountifully! If God's people obeyed, they would have more resources to carry out His plans. They would be more effective. Why? The seventh year rested the land, but it also rested the people.

A Matter of Faith

Rest is the fundamental physical issue in God's Sabbath cycle. To maintain the health of the land and of the people, God ordered rest. However, the primary *spiritual* issue is faith.

Why did God command that His people obey the Sabbath laws for the seventh day, the seventh year, and the year of jubilee (Lev. 25:8-12)? **He was testing the faith of His people!** Obedience demonstrated that they trusted God. Disobedience showed they did not. God wanted to prove that He could meet their needs without their planting and harvesting efforts. It protected them from the wrong dependency. If they could depend on God during six years of work, could they not also depend on Him during one year of rest?

God realized this plan wouldn't make sense to people who only knew how to work the land. In verse 20 He voices their question: "What are we going to eat on the seventh year if we do not sow or gather in our crops?" He knew that His people did not believe they could survive without working!

To make things worse, their survival was not just in question for one year, but two! In the seventh year, they were forbidden not only from harvesting but also from *sowing* (v. 45). They could not gather food in the seventh year, nor would there be a crop to harvest during the eighth year! God was placing them in a position where they had to rely on Him *alone* for their survival for *two whole years.*

When God tests the faith of His people, He always has a plan to take care of them. His plan provided more than what they could have provided for themselves. "I will so order My blessing for you in the sixth year that it will bring forth the crop for *three* years. When you are sowing the eighth year, you can still eat old things from the crop, eating the old until the ninth year when its crop comes in" (vv. 21-22, emphasis added).

Just think, God's resources provided three years of food from one year of work. What an incredible blessing! What an incredible test of faith!

Do you remember that God gave the same challenge during Israel's time in the wilderness? When the miracle manna appeared, the people could gather only one day's nourishment. However, God changed this practice on the sixth day. He ordered that they gather twice as much to prepare for the seventh day rest (Exod. 16:22, 29-30).

These scriptures teach that there are two reasons for the "seventh rest" cycles. First, God designed this cycle to give the human body the rest that it needs. Obeying God's command to rest keeps the body strong to carry out His plan. The second purpose is to remind us to depend only on Him. The Israelites had to trust God to give them extra manna on the sixth day to insure provision for the seventh.

And so it is with us! God tests us to find out whether we really believe that He will take care of *everything* that needs to happen even while we cease toiling to give our bodies the Sabbath they deserve.

There is yet another implication of God's principle of cyclical rest. To disobey His plan brings about consequences He never intended. Nothing illustrates this better than the 70-year Exile that the children of Israel suffered. In Jer. 27 and 29 God predicted the 70-year Babylonian Exile as well as the promised return. Is it simply historical fact that the Israelites spent 70 years in exile? In order to discover the reason for the number of exiled years, we need to return to Levitical law.

Why 70 Years?

As we look at the beginning of Judah's exile, we learn one of God's timeless principles. Jer. 29 includes God's prophecy and promise: "When *seventy years* have been completed for Babylon, I will visit you and fulfill My good word to you, to bring you back to this place" (v. 10, emphasis added). With this statement, God precisely foretells the length of the Babylonian Exile.

God did not make a random choice when He announced this 70-year Exile. The number is significant. To understand why He chose this number, let's consider Levitical law. God's command to His people was clear and explicit. As already explained, God permitted working the land for 6 years but commanded rest for the land and the people during the 7th year. However, at the same time that God gave this sabbatical law, He also predicted that they would disobey it and prophesied the resulting Exile (Lev. 26:31-33). It is what He says next that *directly links* the Exile and sabbatical law. *"Then the land will enjoy its sabbaths* all the days of the desolation, while you are in your enemies' land; *then the land will rest and enjoy its sabbaths.* All the days of its desolation it will observe the rest which it did not observe on your sabbaths, while you were living on it"* (vv. 34-35, emphases added).

Robbing the Land of Sabbaths

When Saul became king, it was the first time that a government leader could enforce sabbatical law by decree. However, because of the disobedient and faithless hearts of the people, neither the 7th year of rest nor the jubilee years were ever observed.[1] Not for the land. Not for the people.

Establishing the time of the beginning of Saul's reign is of major prophetic significance and has profound implications for the Seventh Rest cycles. Based on the undisputed dating of Solomon's death and the dividing of the kingdom in 931 B.C.[2], the beginning of David's 33-year reign in Jerusalem is 1004 B.C.[3] That means his 7-year reign over Judah in Hebron began in 1011 B.C.[4] Saul's reign began 40 years earlier in 1051 B.C. (Acts 13:21).

> The people stole 70 years of rest from the land . . . and . . . God gave the land every one of them back.

The exile of the Jews began 445 years later in 606 B.C. with the first deportation to Babylon.[5]

In any given 50 years, there were 7 sabbatical years and 1 jubilee year. In 400 years, 56 sabbaticals and 8 jubilees would transpire. In the additional 45 years, 6 more sabbaticals would occur. Thus, from the beginning of King Saul's reign until the exile, the years of national disobedience had robbed the land of *70 years of rest.**

Historians tells us that the Exile ended in 536 B.C. when Cyrus of Medo-Persia conquered Babylon and allowed the Jews to return to rebuild the Temple.[6] This is exactly 70 years after it started, just as Jeremiah prophesied (29:10). The Exile gave the land back its sabbaticals, *every last one of them.* Second Chronicles reminds us of this fact: "Therefore He brought up against them the king of the Chaldeans [Nebuchadnezzar]. . . . And those who had escaped from the sword he carried away to Babylon . . . to fulfill the word of the LORD by the mouth of Jeremiah, *until the land had enjoyed its sabbaths.* All the days of its desolation it kept sabbath until *seventy years were complete"* (36:17, 20-21, emphases added).

What Does This Mean to You?

Perhaps you are wondering what this lesson in biblical history has to do with you. I believe that it has deep meaning for all of God's children, but *especially* for those who are called to be ministers of His Word. Our sovereign God created the world with unalterable natural laws. All creation submits to these unchangeable laws (Rom. 8:20). Furthermore, the very foundation of science comes from the fact that **physical occurrences taking place under the same circumstances will produce the same results.** Why? Because God has subjected the entire universe to His order. Thus, scientific "laws" are merely a reflection of the order God created for all things. Indeed, the only reason that the universe does not degrade into random

---

*Although reputable authorities may use different dates for the same events, it does not change the prophecy or the disobedience that caused it.

oblivion today is because God wills it to remain ordered. Science is no more than the continued discovery of the reality that "by Him all things were created, both in the heavens and on earth, visible and invisible . . . *and in Him all things hold together*" (Col. 1:16-17, emphasis added)!

All humanity, both believers and nonbelievers, are subjected to these laws. Let me illustrate. If a Christian and a non-Christian fall from a 500-foot cliff, the law of gravity equally affects both. Both will die a physical death when they hit ground. God does not suspend the law of gravity for someone who becomes a Christian.

Paul says the same thing when he writes, "Creation was subjected to futility" (Rom. 8:20). He goes on to say that even those who experience "the first fruits of the Spirit, *even we ourselves* groan within ourselves, waiting eagerly for our adoption as sons, the redemption of our *body*" (v. 23, emphases added). The impact of God's redemption is twofold: (1) He redeems our souls from eternal punishment; and (2) He redeems our bodies from the futility of subjection to natural laws (v. 20). However, notice that this bodily redemption does not occur until physical death or Christ's return.

The Benefits of Obedience

While there is a consequence for disobedience, there are benefits to obeying. Believers and unbelievers both benefit from obeying God's laws. For example, examine two couples who live in heterosexual, monogamous marital relationships. One couple is Christian, and one is not. Neither couple uses illicit intravenous drugs. Both experience the same protection against contracting AIDS. Both run an equally small risk of infection from the human immunodeficiency virus (HIV). *Both* benefit from obeying God's moral laws against homosexuality (Rom. 1:26-32; 1 Cor. 6:9-10) and against misusing the body (vv. 19-20).

This is one of many ways to illustrate how all humankind is subjected to God's *physical and moral* laws whether they believe in Him or His laws. God's laws affect both the believer and unbeliever. Of course grace makes a difference. By grace, through faith, God pardons believers and rescues them from the **eternal** consequences of sin. However, no one escapes the *physical* consequences of disobeying God's laws. Redeemed souls still live in bodies subject to God's physical laws. Nothing will change this fact except death or the return of our Lord Jesus Christ.

That's where we begin to see the clear and unalterable impact of disobeying the seventh rest. From the beginning, God set in motion a natural law regarding the physical rest of His creation. He imposed it upon Adam and Eve before they had sinful, decaying bodies. In His special relationship with the Jews, He further communicated this concept in His law ordaining a weekly Sabbath, the High Sabbaths, the sabbatical year, and the jubilee system. All mankind faces the same physical consequences for ignoring the cyclical rest God commanded.

This fact is true because the sabbatical law represents a foundational physical law: the body and mind must have regular rest. To relegate this law to a spiritual requirement is to miss its foundational nature. Because it involves a physical truth, the law is true independent of spiritual regeneration, which occurs apart from the law. While there are spiritual consequences for disobeying spiritual laws, there are also physical consequences for ignoring physical laws. The Exile demonstrates both.

> If you don't give your body its Sabbaths, your body's own system of checks and balances will take them back.

The length of the Exile was another way God reminded His people that the land would get its Sabbaths. The Jews stole 70 sabbaticals from the land, and God received every one of them back. If God's people will not give the land its Sabbaths, then God will find a way to restore them. The same is true concerning the Sabbaths that God created your body to enjoy. If you don't give your body its Sabbaths, your body's own system of checks and balances will take them back.

Do not be deceived! The body of the believer is still a decaying earthen vessel (2 Cor. 4:7-10). **The rate at which the body decays is directly related to how one obeys God's natural laws!**

Certainly God still heals. As a medical doctor, I have seen patients healed in ways that can *only* be explained by God's miraculous intervention. However, even the fact that we have the privilege to request supernatural healing from God does not remove our responsibility to obey His natural laws.

The prophet Daniel clearly understood that disobedience to God's law produced consequences. During his exile, Daniel remembered that Jeremiah predicted 70 years of exile (Dan. 9:2). Daniel responds to Jeremiah's prophecy by praying a prayer of corporate repentance for turning away from God's commandments and ordinances (vv. 17-19). He didn't ask God to remove him from captivity at 30 or 40 or even 60 years! He understood that until the land had received back all of its sabbaticals, the nation could not be restored and delivered. He knew that praying for deliverance before that time would have been fruitless.

Keeping the Rhythm of Life

Keeping Sabbath means keeping the rhythm of God-created life. It embraces the full meaning of work and productivity as well as the deepest meaning of body and mind rest. God calls the one who refuses to work lazy. God calls the one who will not rest disobedient.

> God calls the one who will not rest disobedient.

Unfortunately, clergy and laity alike do not pay attention to God's prescribed cycle. A seven-day cycle involving work, worship, and rest protects spiritual and physical health. What I know as a physician is that **your body will get its rest!** Either you can give your body its *Sabbaths,* its time to *cease* and *desist,* or your body will take them back. It's back to choice and decision. There is no exception clause allowing overwork without consequences just because you serve God. Instead, *because* you serve God, you choose to follow His design that includes rest as a predictable part of your seven-day week, just as He prescribed.

God's ways are higher than ours (Isa. 55:9). We do not have the authority to change His plan. It took an exile to give Canaan's soil the 70 years of rest the people had robbed from the land. What will it take for you? If we are unwilling to follow God's plan for recurrent weekly rest and intermittent time away from work, we will pay a price.

Our wisdom says that resting is a waste of time. *Our* wisdom says that we can get more done if we work six and a half days a week. *Our* wisdom says that taking a vacation for a prolonged period of time will compromise God's plan for ministry. And *our* wisdom keeps the time bomb ticking. No matter how righteous, no matter how spiritual, no matter how called we are, God's plan for our lives will never negate His clearly laid out precepts from His eternal Word.

In his book *Pastors at Risk*, H. B. London is very transparent about when he recognized this fact: "Though I do not like to admit it, there were long periods when I didn't take a day off. But that was wrong. I now believe it is a sin against self and family."[7] Indeed, it is a sin against God, our Creator.

Just as the Promised Land received the rest it was due, our bodies also will have their rest. Unfortunately, many believe that ministry involvement exempts them from this obedience. They believe that if their work is spiritual in nature, they will experience a reprieve from the ravages of misuse. Anyone who thinks this way clearly misunderstands our frailty. In fact, George Barna says: "My interaction with older pastors indicates that many of them have worn themselves out by the time they reach 65."[8] What happened to the Calebs who would say that they are as strong at 85 as they were at 40 (Josh. 14:6-11)?

At the Brink of Victory—Disaster

How many pastors are unable to participate in victories because of physical, mental, or spiritual exhaustion? What if the revival you prayed for did not happen because of debilitating disease associated with overwork?

Don't short-circuit God's long-term plans with your short-sightedness. Give your body its Sabbaths and its sabbaticals.

Because of failure to obey God's plan for cyclical rest, the epidemic of ministers leaving their calling, burning out, and experiencing tragic moral failure continues. It is a time bomb in the church that ticks with ever-increasing fallout of ministerial discouragement and dropout. When the time bomb explodes, it exiles ministry leaders in ways God never intended. Just as the exile of Judah was never part of God's plan, neither is an exile from ministry part of God's plan for His servant. It's not a matter of punishment. It's a matter of natural consequence.

> **When the time bomb explodes, it exiles ministry leaders in ways God never intended.**

Reviewing the Test

How do you score on God's weekly tests? Do you take off a full 24 hours in each weekly cycle? Do you trust Him to give you what you need for two days on the sixth day? Do you demonstrate your trust in and dependence on God by allowing Him to do what needs to be done while your body, soul, and spirit enjoy their Sabbaths? Never forget that the seventh rest not only is for your body but also grows and strengthens your faith. It encourages vision. It enables a longer and more effective ministry. Whatever it takes to restore God's plan for cyclical rest, take a step today. Don't wait for your body to take it for you.

What About You?

- Do you connect the Sabbath cycle only with Jewish law or Sunday worship?

- Have you reviewed how God implemented His Sabbath cycle in biblical history?

- Do you understand the physical consequences of ignoring God's prescribed rest?

- Do you take off a full 24 hours in a 7-day week? Can you look at your schedule and plan special seventh week rests?

- Can you consider the possibility of a minisabbatical following six years of ministry?

- To whom are you accountable for this plan?

ENDNOTES

1. R. K. Harrison, Howard F. Vos, C. J. Barber, eds., *The New Unger's Bible Dictionary* (Chicago: Moody Press, 1988), 408.

2. Ibid., 234. See also B. Wilkinson, K. Boa, *Talk Thru the Old Testament* (Nashville: Thomas Nelson Publishers, 1983), 85, 109 and S. Winward, *A Guide to the Prophets* (Atlanta: John Knox Press, 1977), 9.

3. Harrison, et al., *The New Unger's Bible Dictionary,* 234. See also Wilkinson and Boa, *Talk Thru the Old Testament,* 78.

4. Wilkinson and Boa, *Talk Thru the Old Testament,* 78, 85.

5. Ibid., 118. See also G. R. Jeffrey, *Armageddon: Appointment with Destiny* (New York: Bantam Book, 1988), 153-54 and R. Anderson, *The Coming Prince,* 10th ed. (Grand Rapids: Kregel Publications, 1984), 10.

6. Wilkinson and Boa, *Talk Thru the Old Testament,* 118. See also Anderson, *The Coming Prince,* 11 and Jeffrey, *Armageddon: Appointment with Destiny,* 153.

7. H. B. London and Neil B. Wiseman, *Pastors at Risk* (Wheaton, Ill.: Victor Books, 1993), 24.

8. George Barna, *Today's Pastors* (Ventura, Calif.: Regal Books, 1993), 32.

CHAPTER 6

A Booby Trap:
The All Things Complex

While obeying the sabbatical principle is a fundamental part of addressing stress and overwork, there are other issues. One involves the job description for today's multichallenged pastor.

In one day, whether his or her calendar shows it or not, a pastor will be counselor, administrator, financial planner, teacher, employer, church growth expert, janitor, hospital chaplain, arbitrator, and theologian. His or her coatrack doesn't even have enough room for the hats that must be worn. Some of the roles represent areas of strength and interest and are energy producing. Others represent areas of weakness or insecurity and are energy zapping. Balancing the two places the pastor in a precarious predicament and makes such a one very susceptible to stress and exhaustion.

Defining the role of pastor for the 21st century poses no small problem. Just what is a minister supposed to do? And how much of it is he or she supposed to do? Too often pastors fall prey to everybody's expectations. Too many people expect the shepherd to do too many things. Unfortunately, each ministry task is important and usually necessary in achieving the mission of the church. However, unrealistic expectations can be devastating.

A recent study documented how pastors evaluated their specific activities.[1] Their workweek averaged more than 62 hours! Even more significant was that pastors averaged 255 separate work activities, each averaging 15 minutes in length! It's no wonder a pastor feels fragmented and overwhelmed.

So Many Hurting People

It's not just the pastor's fault. There are trends that compound this pastoral problem. A major contributing factor is the sin and depravity of our society. An ever-growing proportion of parishioners are coming to our churches with tremendous hurts, needs, and debilitating scars. They live with the devastating consequences of sin. The one with a shepherd's heart sees those desperate needs and desires to meet them. However, the sheer number and scope of such needs can totally consume even an experienced minister.

Another complication is our society's preoccupation with self. With great subtlety, it has found its way into the church. The servant mentality becomes an uncommon attribute of people who call themselves the children of God. In many cases, this has led to the dismantling of the "need-meeting" capacity of the church. In fact, although there are exceptions, Barna's research has shown a clear trend of decreasing lay volunteer ministry in the church.[2]

In one of Barna's surveys, he asked pastors to identify the greatest difficulty they faced in the church. Nearly one-third identified the lack of commitment among laypersons. Not only was it the number one difficulty identified, but also it was mentioned more than twice as often as any other issue.[3] This points to the pastor's perception of being numbered with a dwindling population of Christians with a sense of responsibility to meet the needs of others. This small group knows that giving the gospel apart from a caring environment will not work (James 2:14-20).

The All Things Complex

Where does this leave a caring pastor? With an increasing number of needs to meet with a decreasing number of people to meet them. Who fills in the gap?

When Paul admonished disciples to be "all things" to all people, he wasn't advocating overwork and burnout. The context for 1 Cor. 9:19-23 is clear. Paul wanted to present the message of the gospel in ways to assure its acceptance. He did this while simultaneously remaining utterly committed to the integrity of the unchanging message of the truth. He said, "I have become all things to all men, *that I may by all means save some. And I do all things for the sake of the gospel*" (vv. 22-23, emphasis added). What Paul did not mean was that he presented himself as the one through whom all the needs of the Body were met.

Instead, the end of this passage reveals that Paul's primary focus always remained winning the lost. He reiterates this in the next chapter: "Whether, then, you eat or drink or whatever you do, do all to the glory of God. Give no offense either to Jews or to Greeks or to the church of God; *just as I also please all men in all things*, not seeking my own profit, but the profit of the many, *that they may be saved*" (10:31-33, emphases added).

The Scripture teaches that the whole Body of Christ should be an effective need-meeting organization. However, Paul's *primary* focus was neither clothing the poor, feeding the hungry, nor healing the sick. Too many people in today's churches expect the pastor to meet all of their physical, emotional, and spiritual needs through the ministry he or she administrates. These expectations have become so great that they often replace their primary calling, *to know God and make Him known!*

A CEO or Prophet?

If this were not enough, we have entered an age in which many view the church as nothing more than a business. Some act as if the "professional" pastor is "hired" by the congregation and treated as an employee. They have lost sight of the special relationship that exists between God and those whom He has set apart for the ministry of the gospel. This biblical concept, which gives the pastor direct spiritual authority and responsibility for the congregation, is profoundly significant. When a congregation views the pastor as one who is paid to meet the needs of the congregation as the congregation determines those needs, it undermines this biblical model. It encourages churches to hire a minister to "baby" the believers. They want a pastor to speak nicely to the congregation from the pulpit and spend the rest of the time taking care of their problems. Speaking as a layman, this is a formula for disaster.

The User-friendly Trap

Compounding the "all things" mentality is the contemporary view that the pastor should provide a user-friendly ministry environment. Clearly there is merit to the biblical aspects of this church growth concept. However, its misuse has given the user-friendly theology a life of its own. Overemphasizing a user-friendly methodology pushes the pastor toward a frantic attempt to meet every "felt need" of the congregation and pushes the pastor away from his or her call to redeem the lost. And what happens to the pastor who does not fit this popular model of universal "need meeter"? That one is misunderstood as lazy, uncaring, or incompetent.

> Overemphasizing a user-friendly methodology pushes the pastor toward a frantic attempt to meet every "felt need" of the congregation and pushes the pastor away from his or her call to redeem the lost.

Nothing could be worse for the pastor or the church. Scripture clearly teaches that the ministry priorities of the pastor/prophet are twofold: to pray and preach the Word of God. A clear biblical basis for this comes from Acts 6. Do you remember the dispute that arose in the Early Church? The Greek Jews complained against the native Jews about equal food distribution to the widows. Somebody's needs weren't being met, and the apostles were supposed to solve the problem.

It is important to remember that the apostles did not consider this a trivial issue. Their Servant-Model had trained them. Jesus himself met many needs. The apostles understood the priority of meeting needs. In fact, Jesus' brother James defined true religion this way: "This is pure and undefiled religion in the sight of our God and Father, to visit orphans and widows in their distress, and to keep oneself unstained by the world" (1:27). Therefore, the apostles felt strongly about the high priority of meeting people's needs within the Body, especially those who were underprivileged or bereaved.

That's what makes the apostles' response to this need so astonishing. In a very clear and straightforward manner, they made known God's priority for their ministry. They told the congregation that they would not neglect the Word of God to serve tables (Acts 6:2). What would happen if you said something like that in your church? Maybe some would respond, "Who do you think you are?" Many might misjudge: "He thinks he's too important to wait tables like us!" Others would ask, "How are we going to grow a church with a pastor who doesn't care about our needs?"

Neglecting Needs or Meeting Priorities?

The apostles were not implying that feeding the widows was unimportant or that distributing food or serving tables was a trivial calling. What they were saying was that it wasn't *their* calling! In fact, they addressed the need by delegating to "seven men of good reputation, full of the Spirit and of wisdom" (v. 3).

With this plan, they did not personally assume the responsibility but responsibly ensured that someone would meet these widows' needs. And they used the church body to do it. This was not a who-needs-to-be-involved appointment. After the men had been chosen, the apostles prayed and laid hands on them (vv. 5-6). What would happen to the understanding of ministry in your church if every job from changing diapers in the nursery to washing dishes in the kitchen began with a similar public prayer of commitment?

This was a perfect opportunity for each of the apostles to become an all-things minister. Had that occurred, it is possible that the congregation would have agreed without protest. Instead, the ministers of the gospel taught the congregation about Jesus' call and priority base.

Jesus' Priority Base

In the high-priestly prayer, Jesus makes an astonishing statement as it relates to meeting needs. Tucked within this tender, compassionate intercession are these words: "[Father,] I glorified Thee on the earth, having accomplished the work *which Thou hast given Me to do"* (John 17:4, emphasis added).

What a staggering testimony! Jesus accomplished everything that the Father gave Him to do. There is a biblical concept here that has profoundly changed my life. In fact, it is foundational for anyone who seeks to follow God's call to ministry. Contrary to what many might think, **Jesus was not need-centered.** People's needs were not the number one priority that influenced the how and when of Jesus' ministry. He did not preach every sermon that He could have preached. He did not heal every disease or infirmity. He did not meet every need.

> **Jesus was not need-centered. . . . Jesus was Father-centered.**

What was His priority base? **Jesus was Father-centered.** The Father said "Preach" and He preached. The Father said "Heal" and He healed. The Father said "Minister" and He ministered. Jesus did not allow the needs of people to set His ministry agenda. He allowed His Father to do that.

When a Christian leader assumes that a need-centered ministry is the same as a Father-centered ministry, this misunderstanding may be a catalyst for a time bomb. It may be the single greatest cause for pastoral overwork, exhaustion, and burnout.

A Need-Meeting Unity

The church's response in Acts 6 fascinates me. After the apostles stated that their primary priorities were to devote themselves to prayer and to the ministry of the Word, the apostles "found approval with the whole congregation" (v. 5). Because they did not compromise God's plan for the church, what began as a dispute ended with resolution. And the resolution found approval with the *whole congregation.*

This passage leads to an interesting question: What if the people had questioned their priorities? Do you think that the apostles would have neglected the Word of God to serve tables? I don't think so. The apostles didn't allow congregations to derail them from God-given responsibilities in other situations. It would not have happened here.

Are You Serving Tables?

As you look at the way you spend your time, have you begun to neglect the Word of God in order to serve tables? When you look at your list of responsibilities, does it reflect a single-minded devotion to prayer and to the ministry of the Word? Of course you are sensitive to your congregation's perceptions. However, whose servant-model will you follow? When God defines your service, He does so in a way to serve the gospel. No one removes your responsibility to obey God's call and submit to His priorities.

Part of the Problem

There are two reasons this passage is so important in our discussion of exhaustion and burnout. First, God has defined a very short list of responsibilities for His appointed spokesmen. The fact that the Barna survey, mentioned earlier, lists so many tasks is one of the *primary* factors leading to exhaustion and burnout in the ministry. The important question each pastor must answer is, Who made the list so long?

The second reason for its importance is to make sure we do not compromise the most fundamental mission of the church. Go back to the sixth chapter of Acts. After the apostles stated their priorities, appointed the seven, and laid hands on them, what happened next? "And the word of God kept on *spreading;* and the number of disciples continued to *increase greatly* in Jerusalem, and a *great many* of the priests were becoming obedient to the faith" (v. 7, emphases added).

Nothing in the Scripture is random or coincidental. Hence, the proximity of these statements has profound meaning. This passage reveals a cause-and-effect relationship between verses

1-6 and verse 7. Because the preachers of the gospel did not neglect the Word of God in order to serve tables and because they devoted themselves to prayer and to the ministry of the Word, God's Word spread. Not only did it spread, but also it was fruitful. The disciples increased and even included the conversion of Jewish priests. In other words, there was revival!

Don't underestimate the obedience connection here. Unity, met needs, and revival all happened *because* the preachers of the gospel did not compromise their God-given priorities. There is serious fallout for disobedience and compromise. The first is obvious. Without the right priorities, preachers of the gospel neglect prayer and the ministry of the Word for other "important" responsibilities. Another consequence from this disobedience is exhaustion, disillusionment, and perhaps burnout. And the consequences continue: the spreading of God's Word to the world is compromised, God's plan for revival is short-circuited, and opposition leaders remain enemies of the faith instead of turning toward God as He had planned.

Fortunately, there is another alternative. When ministers of the gospel focus their ministry on the priorities of prayer and God's Word, many things happen that would not have occurred any other way. The church meets needs, those called to serve experience the joy of service, complaints do not separate, and a divided congregation becomes united (vv. 1-6). However, as important as these things are, the most important result is that the Word of God spreads, disciples increase, and many former enemies of the gospel become obedient to the faith (v. 7).

Do you see the domino effect? One victory led to another. And the first domino was an uncompromising commitment to prayer and the ministry of the Word. Neglecting this priority, even to meet important needs, affects the health of the church and could affect the health of its pastor.

Why Do You Preach?

Do you remember the first time you experienced your call to preach? Does that call still anchor every part of your ministry? Is your calling so real that you would preach the Word until your last breath? Can you testify with Paul: "I am under compulsion; *for woe is me if I do not preach the gospel*"? (1 Cor. 9:16, emphasis added). That call, while it represents a way to support your family, goes beyond financial payment. God's plan includes that His call gives you a way to support your family while allowing you to devote yourself completely and wholeheartedly to your call (vv. 6-14, 18; 1 Tim. 5:17-18; Matt. 10:9-10; Luke 10:7).

Who Called You?

If your call came from any other source but God, it makes you vulnerable to other pulls and tugs that do not come from Him. It pressures you to fit into other people's expectations. To fill the gaps. To be all things. To work to the point of exhaustion. To misorder priorities. To burn out.

On the other hand, a call from God gives balance to your schedule. It defines your "reasonable service" (Rom. 12:1, KJV) in ways that do not shortchange your family. It does not allow other people's expectations or popular ministry philosophies to deter you from your divine call! It does not mean there is no resistance from others. It means that as you concentrate on the ministry of the Word, people will not be able to reject the biblical model you follow. They will support your obedience and reexamine their own.

Please understand that this commitment does not reject accountability. God's ordained leaders cannot remove themselves from accountability to their congregations. A pastor must be accountable to his or her lay leaders. But it is the pastor's responsibility to teach a congregation about proper, biblically founded, God-given priorities. And as the church responds to such biblical leadership, those who are led by the Holy Spirit will rise to the responsibility of meeting other needs in the Body. That's the biblical model. Let the other parts of the Body do their tasks of service, and you do yours (Rom. 12:3-8; Eph. 4:11-12). Mixing them up is a formula for burnout.

What the World Needs Most

In this self-centered day, many in the church are blinded to what they really need! When asked, they'll be happy to supply an enormous list of what they *think* they need. Such a list will contain things such as money, leisure, possessions, a counselor, more programs, fewer programs, therapy sessions, financial guidance, and a whole host of other "essential" needs. They believe that complete satisfaction will happen when all their needs are met. But the Word of God teaches that there is only one thing that makes men free. There is only one thing that leads men to the answers for their deepest and most desperate needs. **Only the truth will set men free!** (John 8:31-32). Because of this, a minister's primary role is to speak the truth. It is your occupation; indeed, it must be your preoccupation!

Spurgeon's Prophetic Words

We live in a desperate day. Our society, and sometimes the church, is coming apart at the seams. And why does this unraveling occur? Why does the bondage exist? It comes by compromising the truth and reordering the priorities.

A prophetic message from the great English preacher Charles Haddon Spurgeon more than a century ago still communicates the need for uncompromising commitment to preach the Word.

> It is today as it was in the reformer's days . . . we who have had the Gospel passed to us by martyr hands dare not trifle with it, nor sit by and hear it denied by traitors, who pretend to love it, but inwardly abhor every line of it. The faith I hold bears upon it marks of the blood of my ancestors. Shall I deny their faith, for which they left their native land to sojourn here? Shall we cast away the treasure which was handed to us through the bars of prisons, or came to us charred with . . . flames . . . ?
>
> . . . When I think of how others have suffered for the faith, a little scorn or unkindness seems a mere tri-

fle, not worthy of mention. As for me, I must hold the old Gospel: I can do no other. God helping me, I will endure the consequences of what men think. . . .

Look you, sirs, there are ages yet to come. If the Lord does not speedily appear, there will come another generation, and another, and all these generations will be tainted and injured if we are not faithful to God and to His truth today. We have come to a turning point in the road. If we turn to the right, mayhap our children and our children's children will turn that way; but if we turn to the left, generations yet unborn will curse our names for having been unfaithful to God and His Word.[4]

Minister of the Gospel or Jack-of-All-Trades?

The weight of needs within the church pressures you to be all things to all people. Many times it feels like the church attempts to make you a jack-of-all-trades. However, even before the foundations of the earth, God foreknew His profound call upon your life (Jer. 1:4-5)! Do not waver from this call. Do not shirk your primary responsibility. Do not succumb to the all things complex. It is a booby trap that will explode when you least expect it. Obey your call. Be a minister of the gospel!

WHAT ABOUT YOU?

- Have you defined realistic responsibilities?
- Do you allow the weight of needs to change God-ordered priorities?
- Do you fill in the gaps for other people's lack of commitment?
- Do you practice biblical accountability?
- Do you still sense God's call to preach the Word?
- Do you commit priority time to prayer?
- Have you tried to be all things and struggled with emotional or physical exhaustion or both when you cannot?

ENDNOTES

1. R. Ryding, Ph.D. diss., Vanderbilt University; in Mark Graham, "Chestnut Ridge—a Ministry for Ministers," *Herald of Holiness,* June 1995, 11.

2. George Barna, *What Americans Believe* (Ventura, Calif.: Regal Books, 1991), 64-70, 242-44.

3. Ibid., 65-66.

4. Charles H. Spurgeon, "Holding Fast the Faith," in *The Metropolitan Tabernacle Pulpit,* vol. 34 (London: Passmore and Alabaster, 1888), 83-84.

CHAPTER 7

Wired for Disaster: Relational Isolation

After seminary, Randy and Elaine were filled with so much excitement over their first church that they didn't even notice when church people kept them at arm's distance in relationships. At their second church, they found themselves reaching for more relationships, especially the ones that met their children's friendship needs. That was when they confronted the perception that a pastor's family couldn't have special friends. Not wanting to disturb unity, they pulled back from relationships, made social appearances, listened to everybody else's needs, and never confessed their own. By the third and fourth church, this was just second nature. They had convinced themselves that the pastor's family couldn't afford the luxury of intimate friendships. However, when one of their children hit the rebellious teen years at full speed and Elaine's father died and Randy's mother developed Alzheimer's, their unsupported world began to fall apart. Not only did they feel isolated, but also they began to feel that no one cared about their pain. As they pushed more and more pain inside, they lost perspective and enthusiasm, began to experience more and more health issues, and finally came to wonder why they were in ministry at all. Believing it to be a sign indicating their need for a change, they began looking at other options for the rest of their life.

As a pastor, your needs are no different from the rest of the world when it comes to support. You need nurturing relationships. You need intimate friendships. You need a support system already in place when hard times occur. This is not an option for ministry effectiveness; it is a prerequisite.

As a medical doctor, I pay attention to research that enables me to provide the best possible help for patients. Recently, I came across a significant body of research that reveals what all of us should have known. It is simply that the quality of one's relational support system directly affects the occurrence of health problems. Over and over the studies show that people with good social support systems have a decreased risk for disease. Even when illness strikes, people with support systems fare much better than those without support systems.

The reverse is also true. People without access to a support system increase their risk of developing a medical problem that could lead to death. One researcher studied a group of elderly people and found that when they had access to human interaction, it reduced the death rate by one-third.

Other studies reveal that a good support system decreases the likelihood of complications in pregnancy, decreases emotional and psychiatric problems, decreases the amount of medication required to control asthma, and decreases arthritis symptoms by affecting fewer joints.

Relationships and the Immune System

Why is this true? Part of the answer lies in the interaction between the immune system, stress, and emotional support from personal relationships. Several investigations have evaluated the impact of stress associated with normal daily activity on the human immune system. They reveal some striking findings. For instance, a study involving medical students who were taking multiple examinations reported that they had a substantially lower white blood cell count. White blood cells are an integral part of the immune system and help kill the germs that cause disease. These students also showed lowered interferon production. Interferon is a natural chemical in the body that helps fight infection. Interestingly enough, this suppression was greater among students who were isolated, who did not maintain supportive relationships, or who felt alienated by other students.

Relational Separation

Physical consequences also occur when relationships are interrupted through death or separation. Researchers who study human responses to bereavement and relational separation have found physical results that include changes in hormonal balance as well as changes in the immune system. As a pastor, you have probably seen some of these changes as you have ministered to people in grief recovery. Just when a bereaved person seems to be getting back to a normal routine, illness hits and hits hard. As a pastor, do you understand that this same susceptibility is yours when you function without the help of significant relationships?

Our mobile society produces its share of relational separation. Rather than staying in one area or region for the greater part of their lives, many people move multiple times. Every geographic move changes and disrupts relationships. In fact, a study investigating the physical effects of rapid change and geographic mobility revealed that such moves can dramatically increase the rate of coronary artery disease. What does this say to the average minister who moves once every three to five years? It says that you run a greater risk for disease unless you learn how to reestablish a support system.

Work and Relational Isolation

Working conditions also affect relationships. The heavier and longer the workweek, the harder it is to develop and maintain relationships. A certain kind of social isolation occurs that may have nothing to do with personality. Without the time or energy to apply to relationships, people opt for TV, videos, and other stay-at-home activities.

Again research studies deliver a powerful message. Studies report that there is an increase of coronary artery disease for those with heavy workloads. Studies also demonstrate that the worker can decrease the negative effects of these working conditions if the person has good personal relationships. That means that workers with an effective social support structure can decrease health complications stemming from overwork or lack of control over the workload.

The Isolation Expectation

Unfortunately, many ministers believe that the very thing that research says can improve health can hurt their ministry. They function under the perception that a pastor cannot afford close relationships with people within the church. Dr. Archibald Hart, in his book *Coping with Depression in the Ministry and Other Helping Professions,* discusses the pastor's lack of friendships as a contributing factor of emotional distress and depression.[1]

Ministers give many reasons for their lack of close relationships. Many believe it interferes with the role of pastor. They fear that if they develop close friendships with some, other parishioners will feel left out. Thus, to prevent hurting anyone's feelings, the parsonage couple deny themselves close friendships. Sometimes pastors fear that close relationships reveal their weaknesses and make them appear ineffective or incompetent.

Even relationships with other pastors don't always address this need for relationship because many do not know how to build a relationship without incurring comparisons or hiding insecurities. Sadly, the ones who need the relationships the most achieve them the least.

Isolation and the Pastor's Family

Unfortunately, the stresses of the modern pastorate contribute to isolation between the husband and wife and members of their immediate family. The isolation I am talking about is not of an extreme nature that leads to divorce or moral failure. Nor am I talking about the isolation that occurs when parents face rebellion in one of their children. It is a much more subtle relational isolation because it occurs in what all would call a *normal* pastor's family.

Let's look at Gail as an example. She married her husband, knowing he was going into the ministry. She believed her marriage vow was as much a vow to love, honor, and support the ministry as the minister. She didn't realize how many nights at home alone it would mean. She didn't expect someone else's needs to take priority over hers. She tried to understand. However, the more that church pressures took her husband away, the more alone she felt in her very peopled world. Who could she share this gnawing loneliness with? Not with the Bible study group she taught. Not with her tired husband at the end of a very busy day. Not with anyone. The more she hid her loneliness, the lonelier she felt. The darkness crept in slowly until she could not get out of bed. Fearing illness, she agreed to tests that all came back negative. Then she saw the counselor who helped her identify her depression.

When a minister's spouse experiences loneliness or depression, she hesitates to share it with anyone. She doesn't want to draw her husband's attention away from the ministry. She copes, or at least tries to. She can keep the masquerade going long enough so that the original cause of the loneliness or depression is buried under other stresses and complications. Obviously, not all ministry spouses are female. However, the same isolation trap exists for the male spouse.

Children can experience the same feeling. The life of a preacher's kid can be very lonely. How well I know, since I am one. There's the pressure to be the good kid, sometimes the model kid. But preachers' kids want to be treated just like other kids. Too much special attention can isolate just as not enough attention. While the parsonage schedule may not be any more chaotic or unpredictable than other homes, the pressure to be at your best in public situations gives little room for normalcy. It's just another form of relational isolation.

This leads to an unfortunate paradox. Despite being surrounded by many loving people, the pastor's family feels isolated! In fact, a 1991 survey of pastors conducted by the Fuller Institute of Church Growth found that "70% of pastors state that they do not have someone they consider a close friend."[2] Then, when the pastor and family try to cope with church pressures and expectations, the dilemma snowballs, rolling down the ministry landscape, collecting other complications, including health issues. The problem is that outward appearances do not reveal their need for support. No one notices the isolation, not even the pastoral family themselves. It sets the scene for a time bomb.

Stress Scoring and Relationships

There are several stress scoring tools available to rate the potential impact of cumulative stress in a person's life. One of them, the Social Readjustment Rating Questionnaire, appears in chapter 2. Other examples include the Life Changes and Illness Model and the Schedule of Recent Events. It is interesting to note that some of the most high-risk stressors in these scales relate to disrupted personal relationships through death, divorce, relocation, and so on.

Research Relevancy

What does all this research mean for the minister? It means that relationships—positive and affirming relationships—are crucial to maintaining mental and physical health. It means that relationships offer a powerful barrier against many diseases. It means that when such relationships are absent or disrupted, this may become a direct factor in the development of illness. It means that when ministers, or anyone else, make choices that prevent close relationships, they risk bearing the full brunt of medical complications from heavy workloads.

If supportive relationships are essential to good health as research shows, how does a minister establish these relationships without compromising the role of pastor? The first answer is to look to the closest relationship available. For most ministers, that means a marriage relationship.

The First Line of Defense

No one would argue that the first line of defense against relational isolation is a good marriage. Unfortunately, the pastor's marriage fits a "high risk" category because of the limited time a husband and wife spend in meaningful interaction.

Even if a husband and wife spend time together, the focus of the time often centers on church schedule, ministry obligations, or family, not the marriage relationship. Overwork and fatigue renders each spouse unable to place relationship before schedule. As a result, a husband and wife may not receive the relational protection that marriage was created to provide. This strains the marriage and actually begins a deterioration, even if there are no outward signs of stress. Over time, the stress renders the relationship too weak to deal with honest needs and transparent insecurities. As a result, it places both partners at an increased risk for many health problems. The pastor and family need the relational protection an honest and interactive marriage provides. It is the best way to protect against the effects of overwork and stress.

Look at your schedule right now. How does it *show* that your marriage is a priority relationship? It won't just happen. It takes time—regular, planned time. If I could write one prescription that could make more difference in your long-term health prognosis, it would simply be to make your marriage a priority and to develop the communication skills that allow each partner to share the wounds and the wishes of the heart.

Making Changes

Whether you are part of the 70 percent of pastors identified in the Fuller study or not, it is clear that pastors are at significant risk for relational isolation and loneliness. It is not something you can ignore. The consequences won't let you. So what *can* you do? Consider some of the following suggestions. Some you can apply today. Others require a perspective and lifestyle change:

1. Take time to relate to your spouse on nonministry issues.

While each of you will talk about your ministry involvements, don't let it consume your time together. Specifically guide communication into areas of mutual interest that have nothing to do with the church. Make sure each of you has time to share how you feel. These are the issues that produce closeness.

2. Plan family activities that provide time to talk together.

Activities such as walking, hiking, cycling, picnicking, camping, and playing table games are just a few of the ones that I remember drew our family together. However, the most important time was mealtime. My parents were always home for supper. It was always a time for affirming communication, laughter, and devotions. This was essential bonding time for our family. If a mealtime doesn't work for you, experiment with something until you find what works.

3. Find a pastor to be your prayer partner.

Another pastor can identify with your stresses. You can discuss things that you can't talk about with your own parishioners. This can provide great support because there is much help in knowing that others fight, and win, similar battles.

4. Make close friendships with a few key laypersons in your congregation.

In the same way a company president may socialize with associates outside of the office, the pastor can develop social relationships outside of church activities. The relationship doesn't focus on church business but on family and common interests. When the relationship happens on personal time and away from church activities, it really shouldn't compromise your ministry relationships.

> **Jesus modeled close relationships for us.**

Besides, Jesus modeled close relationships for us. He ministered to many and related closely to a few. Anyone who says that you can't have close friends in the pastorate rejects Jesus' model. What you can't have is a relationship within the ministry circle to push your agenda about church issues or that appears exclusive while you are with others in the congregation.

5. Frequently remind yourself that close friendships are an important part of maintaining your health.

Never forget that anything that compromises God's plan for health will also compromise His plan for your ministry. Your health is *directly* linked to the successful accomplishment of your hopes and dreams for your family and your church.

6. Make a relationship circle.

Write your name in the center of a piece of paper. Draw a circle around your name. Write the name of your spouse on this circle. Draw another circle, and place the names of your family members around this circle. Draw a third circle. Write the names of two or three people you consider to be your close friends, with whom you can share your deepest feelings and needs. One of these should be a pastor. If you do not have three names, write the names of three you will try to develop. Now draw a line between your circle and the others. Commit to emphasize the importance of these relationships in your life. Then, for the next month, write down what you will do to cultivate relationship within your family and with these two or three people. At the end of this time, evaluate the results and make adjustments.

Not an Option

Research unmistakably demonstrates the health dangers inherent in relational isolation. While many accept a certain amount of isolation as an unavoidable part of ministry, it doesn't have to be. Balance is the key. Don't wait until some health crisis raises its head to underline your need for close relationships.

God created humanity for relationship with Him. Is it any surprise that He created us with a need to relate to each other as well? While God's call sets you apart for ministry, He never intended it to isolate you. Meeting God's created need for relationship is an effective strategy for defusing a hidden time bomb. It will help you protect your marriage and your family. It will provide important protection against unnecessary disease and illness. You will be a more effective channel for God to use in His plan to redeem His world. What could be more successful than that!

WHAT ABOUT YOU?

- **Does your marriage focus on church and ministry, or on building an intimate relationship?**

- Do you take time to talk with your children and make time to do things they like?

- Does your work schedule leave you without time or energy for other relationships?

- Do you know how to reestablish relationships when you move?

- Do you share the perception that a minister cannot have close relationships?

- Are you a part of the 70 percent pastor group who do not have a close friend?

- Will you make changes in perceptions and lifestyle that will protect you and your family from relational isolation?

ENDNOTES

1. Archibald Hart, *Coping with Depression in the Ministry and Other Helping Professions* (Dallas: Word Publishing, 1984), 17.

2. H. B. London and Neil B. Wiseman, *Pastors at Risk* (Wheaton, Ill.: Victor Books, 1993), 22.

CHAPTER 8

Leaving and Grieving

I just received word that a pastor friend of mine is moving. He and his family close a successful chapter of ministry to move to a new church and, I expect, another successful chapter. However, I am aware that this announcement is only a small part of a process that involves change, anxiety, excitement, as well as grief.

First there is the decision process. Balancing pros and cons and listening intently for God's voice finally give way to the euphoria of new challenge. Then reality hits when the pastor makes the first announcement to church leadership and congregation.

Try as they may, it is difficult for a congregation to process a pastor's excitement and their new loss. A string of special occasions and last meals rehearse memories and affirm strengths. Packing boxes fill corners and line walls. The moving truck comes to take everything but the memories. And then it is all new. People. Places. Traditions. Schools. Grocery stores. The welcoming celebrations begin before the just-moved family could possibly have recovered from all their loss. Buried somewhere in the weeks and months to follow could be a fallout—physical, emotional, or even spiritual. It's another time bomb.

Next to death and divorce, moves require people to process more loss than any other change that occurs in the life of a family. Loss means grief. Grief requires time to heal. But where in the chronology of pastoral change is there time to grieve? A new church waits. A new congregation celebrates. No one reserves time to grieve.

Moves and Relational Loss

Numerous scientific studies reveal that changes in one's social or relational circle dramatically increase the risk for disease and ill health. In fact, rapid changes in these areas have been associated with coronary artery disease, heart attack, high blood pressure, and many other health problems.

Relocating your family disrupts relationships and routines and profoundly changes the social structure that provides a family with familiarity and a sense of security. This change substantially impacts emotions, mind, and body. When moves occur frequently, this disruption continues to affect the social stability of your family and leaves them vulnerable to dealing with this stress in physical ways.[1]

> While time heals, time will not grieve for you.

So what is the best way to deal with significant loss so that the pastor and family are ready for the challenges of making a move? While time heals, time will not grieve for you. That's personal work each must do for himself or herself.

The Grief Response

Grief is the important process that acknowledges and works through loss of any kind. Everybody goes through periods of sadness. Something more serious than sadness occurs when someone experiences substantial loss. Even Spirit-filled people get depressed. It is entirely normal when dealing with significant loss. It's just not normal to stay depressed for long periods of time.

Numerous models describe the multiple emotional stages people may go through when they experience loss or separation. Since grief is always unique and personal, no one can accurately predict the stages a person might go through. However, there are three basic components to most grief processes.

Shock. Feelings of denial or disbelief often accompany this part of the grief cycle. The denial may involve any part of the loss and not just the loss itself. This part of grief may last several weeks.

Despair. Disbelief gives way to sadness when the person becomes fully aware of the loss or separation. This is the time a person experiences the full brunt of emotional pain involved. Depending on the loss, feelings of sadness or despair or both can last or reappear for up to a year.

Resolution. This stage of grief is a process that brings closure to the loss. The end of this stage means that a person has accepted the loss and its implications. Resolution generally occurs over several months, and the entire grief process normally takes one to two years.

How does this grief cycle apply to pastoral change? Entertaining the first thoughts of a move begins a realization that change is on the way. The denial or disbelief that characterizes this stage encompasses any part of the move. There is the denial that a move *needs* to happen or disbelief that it will occur. It can even involve denying the financial realities that moves incur.

Often it is family members, especially children, who display more tangible evidences of this first stage of shock. However, anything that causes dramatic change incurs loss, even hidden loss.

The real implications of the loss do not register for several weeks and sometimes several months. It is easy to postpone dealing with the loss from a move as a pastor immerses himself in the new church and its myriad of responsibilities. It is even easier to expect that since a pastor goes from people to people, saying good-bye finishes the grief work.

But it doesn't. The relational loss that occurs during relocation is often significant enough to cause sorrow and grief. It produces major emotional and physical stress. It takes a toll that can even lead to disease and ill health in some situations. It is well documented that the failure to allow people to experience the normal process of grief can lead to significant psychological and medical complications.

A Documented Problem

No one disputes what numerous investigations verify: that

moving a family is a highly stressful event. The corporate world identified this some time ago and has responded with a broad scope of support services for the families of relocated employees. Anderson and Stark extensively evaluated the stresses involved in job relocation. They found that family support services during relocation actually *reduced* job-related illness. These services also *decreased* employee attrition subsequent to relocation.

The belief seems to be that if the move is God's will, then the shock of stage one immediately gives way to resolution in stage three.

Despite these recent findings in the secular work environment, it appears that the stresses of ministry are not well recognized because support services are often nonexistent for pastors.[2] In fact, one study surveyed 28 denominations of more than 200,000 members. Only one denomination provided support services to help the pastoral family adjust to relocation.[3]

A Unique Problem

Some would say that frequent relocation is not unique to the pastoral family in this transient society of ours. This is true. However, there is an aspect of pastoral relocation that is unique and not experienced by laypersons when they move their families. The public nature of a pastor's family move forces them to abbreviate the grief process. Although most parishioners allow the pastoral family a limited time to express shock (stage one), they do not expect them to experience the despair or sadness (stage two) resulting from relational disruption. Or they accept it in the children who have left school and church friends, but not in their pastor or spouse. The church family believes that when the move is God's will, then the shock of stage one immediately gives way to resolution in stage three. No one expects the pastor and his family to be adjusting to relational loss a year after their move. Yet research clearly identifies how irrational that belief is.

To make things more complicated, pastors continue to feel the urgency of their calling, despite separation from friends and familiar surroundings. They often have the same expectations as those around them. They plunge themselves deeply into their ministry to combat feelings of displacement. Unfortunately, the process itself denies the need for grief resolution and keeps them too long in stage one of the grief cycle (shock and denial). The pastoral couple and their new parishioners seem to believe that forgetting the former things is the spiritual thing to do.

Don't Let Us See You Grieve

Our society demonstrates great discomfort when dealing with grief. No one knows what to say or how to say it. Awkwardness often gives way to silence. Silence sends a wrong message. The people needing comfort and understanding often feel isolated.

How does that translate in the world of pastoral moves? Consider the contrast between how a pastor's family and a lay family have permission to talk about a move. When a lay family moves, no one questions comments about missing the old neighborhood or special friendships or even some favorite detail about the home they left. Can a new pastor talk about what he or she misses most about the last pastorate, home, or community? Probably not. People interpret such comments as questioning God's leadership or hanging on to the past or as spiritual immaturity. No one labels it as a healthy part of grief. No one encourages such talk. And the silence participates in shortchanging the grief cycle in ways that add to the stresses of relocation.

It's also the new that has the possibility of overwhelming a family who has just moved. Everything is new: the people, the church, the challenge, the climate, the house, the schools, and the geography. The pastor and family are expected to accept the new with great enthusiasm and excitement. However, when everything is new, it accentuates loss, even when the new is good and God-ordained.

Especially when there has been a long interim between pastors, the new congregation is ready to move on. Unlike their new pastor, they usually had more time to grieve their loss. Without meaning to, the new church family assumes that the pastor intersects the grief cycle at the same place where they are: at the point of resolution. Unfortunately, this assumption pushes the pastor and family to hide or deny their grief. It isolates them in ways that no one intended. It prolongs the grief process, or it creates the kind of stress that results in physical problems or ill health. When a pastor and family move as often as the national average indicates, this short-changed grief process overlaps and creates layers of unfinished emotional business that tick away as a time bomb.

Without meaning to, the new church family assumes that the pastor intersects the grief cycle at the same place where they are: at the point of resolution.

A Setup for Disaster

Why is the discussion of the grief process so important? Because anyone who fails to work through the entire grief cycle is asking for trouble. In fact, Dr. Herbert Weiner states that "the consequences of not being permitted or encouraged to express grief may be dire." He goes on to describe the potential results of short-circuiting this process. These results include feelings of shame, depression, symptoms of ill health, the potential need for prescription medications, resorting to illicit drugs, or even attempting suicide. Pastors are not exempt from experiencing grief from loss just because they follow God to a new place of ministry. Consequently, the failure to work through the grief process can become a dangerous setup for disaster.

Are Christians Supposed to Grieve?

What is the Christian response to loss, especially loss that comes as a direct result of following God's will? Some might say that these scientific investigations relate more to non-Christians than to Christians. After all, aren't Christians, especially God-called ministers, protected in Christ from such grief? On the contrary, there is overwhelming biblical evidence that a grief process is normal. Our relationship with our Heavenly Father does not remove our humanity.

Even as new creatures in Christ, we remain entirely susceptible to emotional and physical suffering. It is a blatant misunderstanding to believe that we should no longer experience grief after coming to know Christ! In the second chapter of Philippians, Paul communicated his great relief that his close friend Epaphroditus did not die from a severe illness that he had suffered. Paul went on to tell us that, if Epaphroditus had died, he would have experienced *"sorrow upon sorrow"* (v. 27, emphasis added). What better example do we have than King David, who taught us through the Psalms that we must come to God open and honest about our feelings during times of grief and depression (69:1-15).

Certainly, after conversion a Christian does view the incidents that cause grief from a different perspective. Growth in Christ produces a foundation of trust in an omnipotent, omniscient God who is in control of the universe. This is a powerful aid in the resolution of grief. But it is also important to remember that God has given grief as one of His healing agents during difficult times. Thus, we must not ignore it in an attempt to be superhuman (or superspiritual).

No one means to postpone or complicate a healthy grief process. However, church people may encourage unhealthy practices that repress grief. These same people would never dream of encouraging an unhealthy practice such as smoking. Many simply aren't aware of how the grief process is an important healing agent to protect against ill health and disease. They simply do not recognize the signs of silent or hidden pain.

Rest Your Grief

Even in the best of circumstances, the life of the pastor is difficult. Add the complexities of a move, and these difficulties escalate. Dealing with so much new as well as loss is very fatiguing. It is easy to deny the fatigue in the middle of experiencing energy surges from the new challenge. It encourages the same stress-induced analgesia discussed in chapter 2.

In addition to acknowledging loss and its implications, there is another very important way to encourage healthy grief work. Rest. Leave the office with unfinished work. Take a nap. Get plenty of regular sleep. Consider getting more sleep than usual for a while. Don't neglect your day off in the first critical weeks of a new assignment. It is vital in moving you toward full resolution in the grief process.

> Don't neglect your day off in the first critical weeks of a new assignment.

Time to Heal

Rest is not the only answer. There are several steps you can take to help avoid the emotional and physical complications described in this chapter:

1. Before leaving a ministry assignment, bring healthy closure to key relationships.

This closure to key relationships includes several factors. Maybe there are people with whom you have had difficulty or a misunderstanding. Ask God for His direction. God may lead you to reconcile your differences. Without question, He will enable you to forgive. The same words you have given to others apply to you: God holds you responsible for *your* attitudes and reactions, not for someone else's. Even if restoration doesn't occur, your heart will be clear. That will protect you from carrying unnecessary baggage into your new assignment.

Closure to key relationships also includes those who have depended on you for their spiritual growth. For some you may be the spiritual parent who introduced them to new life in Christ. They may feel abandoned, as if their spiritual formation depended solely on you. If possible, connect these people with another mature Christian who can help to fill the relational void you will leave in their lives. Use this separation to encourage them toward a new level of spiritual maturity as they connect with another mentor. It will also protect you from feeling that you have abandoned them.

Take time with your closest friends. Express your pain in

leaving a relationship that has nurtured and supported you during your ministry with them. Tell them you will miss them. Tell them how much you love them. Paul models this important part of the leaving and grieving cycle. His letters are full of tender expressions of grief over the necessary separation that his ministry or imprisonment imposed. Healthy closure to relationships doesn't shut the door to future involvement. It changes the context for the relationship. No longer will it connect to local church ministry. Understanding this implication will mean that you go from being pastor-friend to becoming a friend who pastors. Closure of this kind will prepare you and them for the many changes ahead.

2. Take sufficient time off between pastorates.

You need time for rest and emotional transition when you move from one ministry assignment to the next. This is true whether you perceive the need or not. Use this time to draw close to your spouse and children. Share your feelings with them personally, with openness and honesty. Reject the urge to be "strong." It's unhealthy to pretend to your children or spouse that you do not experience any sadness from loss. Besides, your honesty will give others around you permission to express their feelings of loss, pain, loneliness, or anger.

When our family went through our second and final relocation, it was devastating to my brother. He was in high school and wanted to stay behind to finish the second half of the school year. My parents did not believe this was a good decision. However, they also knew how much pain he was experiencing. I vividly remember how they cried *with him* and expressed their own feelings of loss. Because my family chose to work through each stage of grief, they were ready for what was one of the greatest chapters in our family's life. Even my brother looks back on the years in the next church with fond memories! Taking sufficient time off between pastorates will aid in the transition and help prepare you and your family for the new relationships and responsibilities.

3. Give yourself permission to grieve in your new pastorate.

Do this grieving even if those around you do not encourage it. Share your feelings openly with a new friend that you can trust. Then express your grief with one or two key leaders. Hiding your feelings and the humanity they represent is *not* the "spiritual" thing to do! King David and Paul were willing to write about their grief in ways that made it public knowledge. Millions still read of their sorrows. Why don't you express yours to at least a few?

> Understand the difference between grieving loss and comparing churches.

Understand the difference between grieving loss and comparing churches. Making comparisons may signal your need to grieve a loss, but it is not a part of grief work. Not only can the difference create misunderstandings in your new assignment, but also it can postpone dealing with the real grief. The real grief is the fact that something that gave you pleasure, fulfillment, or nurture is gone. Comparison is a backdoor way to tell someone else what you miss. Unfortunately, it creates more ill will than understanding.

In your new pastorate, form relationships with people who will allow you to express grief without condemning you. While it isn't wise to publicly broadcast your sadness over loss, you should look for those who have compassion and patience and can keep a confidence. As you open up to them, they will provide meaningful support for you and your family. Let them know when you're hurting, when you're lonely, or when your spirit is suffering. Give them the chance to help you heal. You will become a stronger ministry team if you do.

4. Become familiar with the normal stages of grief to help you identify where you are in the cycle.

Review the stages of shock, despair, and resolution. Examine more detailed models. Identify your place in the cycle. Don't take shortcuts! Allow God to use grief as His healing agent. It will bring healthy resolution to your spirit, mind, and body, in His time.

5. Don't bury your feelings under work in your new ministry.
What you face in a new pastorate seems to demand all of your waking hours. However, responding to this sense of urgency can be harmful to you and your family. Remember, this is a time in your life when you are very vulnerable, spiritually, physically, and emotionally. Do not waver in your dedication to take your day off each week. Plan time away from your ministry tasks. And when you take time off, spend much of it with your family. Slow down enough for them to share how they are dealing with their losses and coping with all of the new.

In the future, if God's call requires you to relocate, remember: Bring healthy closure to key relationships; take sufficient time off between pastorates; give yourself permission to grieve; understand the normal grief process and identify where you are in the cycle; and, don't bury your feelings with work. Following this plan will minimize the spiritual, emotional, and physical damage to you and your family. It will allow you to experience God's healing. It will prevent a time bomb explosion. It will enable you to be the pastor God called you to be.

WHAT ABOUT YOU?

- Do you know how to identify and allow a grief response for times of loss in your life?

- Is there "unfinished business" in churches you have left?

- Does God want to free you by helping you to apply His principles for reconciliation?

- Are you comparing churches instead of grieving in a healthy manner?

- Do you understand the need to give yourself and your family adequate time to grieve the loss of relationships and familiarity in a move?

- Do you believe that the energy and challenge of a new ministry removes your need to grieve?

- Do you need to talk to your family about any misunderstanding you have had about their need to grieve?

- How will you handle leaving and grieving differently based on this chapter?

ENDNOTES

1. P. W. Blanton, "Stress in Clergy Families: Managing Work and Family Demands," *Family Process* 26 (1992): 315-30.

2. B. Gilbert, *Who Ministers to Ministers?* (New York: Alban Institute, 1987).

3. M. L. Morris and P. W. Blanton, "Denomination Perceptions of Stress and the Provision of Support Services for Clergy Families," *Pastoral Psychology* 42 (1994): 345-64.

CHAPTER 9

A Risky Business

I was meeting with other leaders from my local church. We were reviewing the health-care benefits for the pastoral staff. I looked at the figures representing premium payments, and I thought there was a mistake. They couldn't possibly be this high. After all, we insured our pastors through a denominational plan,[1] expecting to lower premium costs. When I questioned the figures, those meeting with me confirmed them to be accurate.

As a physician, I'm very aware that health-care costs are on the rise. I know that insurance premiums cost more than they did 10 years ago. What I did not know was that pastors, when insured as a group, may pay premiums that are *three times greater* than the average. To say it concerned me is an understatement. Just what does this statistic say to us?

Health-Care Costs

Most health economists would agree with the assumption that health-care costs can be used to approximate the occurrence of ill health and disease in a population. For example, it is well known that overall health-care costs among smokers are dramatically higher than for nonsmokers. This reflects the increased incidence of disease in this group.

In my own Evangelical denomination, many of the over 10,000 pastors are insured through a denominational health-care program. This self-insurance plan generates no profit. Essentially all of the proceeds go to pay for the health care for its members. A small percentage goes to administrate the program. Shouldn't this strategy *lower* health-care costs? It doesn't.

This surprised me because I could think of three reasons why this health plan should cost *less* than individual programs on the market. (1) The large group buying the plan should be able to lower costs. (2) Its nonprofit status should lower costs. (3) Insuring a nonsmoking and nondrinking population should lower the costs. This raised significant red flags for me. What makes pastors as a population group expensive to insure?

They Should Be the Healthiest

Theoretically, one would expect God-called ministers to be one of the *healthiest* populations in our society. It's not that God specifically protects His servants from disease, but He certainly doesn't single them out to experience more ill health and disease than the average person. However, when health-care costs indicate that pastors may be one of the more *unhealthy* population groups and therefore more difficult to insure within average rates, it raises an alarming issue. **Pastors may carry a risk for health problems that is three times greater than the general population.** Why?

At Risk

Much of the answer lies in the issues from previous chapters: stress, exhaustion, too many roles, isolation, and unresolved grief. Add to these factors the escalating demands of people conflict, administration tightropes, recruitment needs, financial crunches, and the ongoing pressure of sermon preparation and other ministry services. No person was created with the capacity to handle demanding pressures without interruption. Like a rubber band stretched beyond its limit, anyone, including ministers, can snap, physically and emotionally.

Stress Causes Change

In chapter 2 we examined some of the physiological abnormalities that stress causes. We found that stress restricts coronary blood flow and can increase the possibility of serious coronary problems, some life threatening. We looked at the adrenaline response necessary to help address physical and emotional stress. We found that continued stress can produce a numbing effect that masks the damage increased stress produces. We looked at a long list of abdominal, digestive, and other disorders that implicate stress. We saw that each of these medical issues signal an alarm to look for the possibility of stress buildup.

Are there specific areas of the pastoral lifestyle that place the minister at risk? I think there are. While no medical research has studied the pastoral lifestyle as a contributing factor to stress, many studies reveal how certain activities, even when they are an expected part of daily routine, cause significant enough stress to produce physical and hormonal changes in the body.

Test Results

Let's start with a simple example. Several research studies show how taking academic examinations substantially increases blood pressure, alters free fatty acid levels, shows a rise in serum cholesterol, and elevations in numerous "stress hormone" levels including insulin, renin, adrenaline, noradrenaline, corticosterone, and growth hormone. Other investigations examine how test taking also lowers white blood cell counts. These cells are an integral part of the immune system and help kill infectious agents (germs). In addition, the research revealed a significant reduction in interferon production, which is a natural chemical in the body that helps fight infection. What stress does to the immune system in some of these testtaking situations is serious enough to cause recurrence of herpes simplex lesions. This virus hibernates and surfaces in stress-related situations. It may have happened to you. Just when you needed to look your best for the dedication of the new building, all the stress for getting to that moment erupts as an ugly cold sore.

Of course if you are not involved in taking tests as a part of ongoing academic work, you might be tempted to disregard these studies as having no application to you. To think this way is to naively miss the point. The point is that many activities exist as a part of a normal work routine that can lead to substantial alterations in bodily functions. If it happens to students who understand examinations as an integral part of their experience, what similar activities produce the same stress levels in ministry? Board meetings? Pastors' reports to superiors? Meeting with a disgruntled member? All of the above.

Public Speaking and Stress

Let's look at another category of research that certainly has more direct application to the life of a minister. Many studies use public speaking as a way to measure the impact of stress on the physical body. Does it surprise you to find out that public speaking leads to substantial neurohormonal changes? These are hormonal changes that affect the neurological system. In many studies adrenaline and its companion noradrenaline showed significant increases during public speaking situations. Interestingly enough, when studies compared the impact of stress of inexperienced speakers to experienced speakers, they recorded changes in the hormone levels of *both* study groups.

These studies, and many others, lead to an important conclusion: The human body endures certain stress that is a normal part of life experience. Even these stresses cause physiologic alterations and damage.

Controlling the Workload

Another example of stress factors inherent in the work environment involves the workload. When a person experiences a stressful situation *in which the person has no control,* cortisol levels show marked elevation. You will recall that elevated cortisol levels can cause high blood pressure and coronary artery disease. *How* many stressful situations do modern ministers face over which they have no control? Continuing to increase cortisol levels leads to other physical implications that may or may not surface as an observable problem for a long time.

Many studies show how working conditions can increase the risk for disease in certain settings. For instance, the risk of coronary artery disease increases as workloads increase. Shift workers who rotate their schedules over long periods of time show an even more dramatic increase in coronary artery disease. Furthermore, workers who do not have stable, predictable work schedules show a risk three times greater than those whose work schedules change very little.

Although none of these investigations relate specifically to overwork in the pastorate, they share important similarities. They tell us that the type of work one does is less relevant than a long pattern of overwork and dramatic shifts in work schedule.

Pastors are well known for long patterns of overwork. The work of ministry never seems to fit neatly between 8 A.M. and 5 P.M.. And ministry workloads are often as unpredictable as the weather. It's feast or famine. While a break in the workload helps, too many unpredictable changes do not. According to the research, overwork and unpredictable work patterns may *dramatically increase* a minister's risk for hypertension, peptic ulcer disease, coronary artery disease, and other health problems.

Pacing Work

The fact that work patterns can impact health is well documented. However, workload is not the only issue involved. For instance, in certain settings, workers have little control over the *pace* of their work. They feel chronically overloaded because they have no ability to voluntarily lower their workload. This situation leads to a higher risk for myocardial infarction (heart attack).

The implications of this study have as much direct relevance to the pastor as if they had studied clergy as a group. It is true that ministers have little or no control over the volume and pace of their work. Administrative decisions often assign work parameters or priorities. In the same way, a stream of people and minicrises interrupt a pastor's already scheduled day. To compensate, a pastor either works longer or harder or goes home frustrated.

Another finding in the study about control and pace of the workload reveals something else relevant to ministry work. When the workload increases, many of the workers in the studies initially responded by investing more emotional energy in their work. They did this as a specific way to gain control. They believed that by working harder they could get ahead of their work. Although initially successful, ultimately this approach to over-work led to emotional distress and frustration.

Those with little control over workload had higher levels of "bad" cholesterol and lower levels of "good" cholesterol.

Tests compared cholesterol levels in these workers with those who were not experiencing frustration over workload. Those with little control over workload had higher levels of low-density lipoprotein more commonly known as "bad" cholesterol and lower levels of high-density lipoprotein or "good" cholesterol. The distressed workers showed an increase in blood pressures as a group. They also demonstrated a higher risk for developing hypertension or high blood pressure as a chronic disease.

A follow-up study evaluated these workers for a three-year period to identify disease and ill health.[2] Researchers compared those who had no control over their workload and its pace to a group who had control. The results document the fact that sleep disturbance was 2.5 times higher and their risk of heart attack was more than *three times greater!*

Lack of control over the amount and pace of work increases frustrations no matter where you work. Ministers face this work issue and because they do, they face significant health risks. Barna's research involving clergy verifies the growing frustrations of a pastor when he says, "Sadly, our research points out that pastors are disappointed with much that is transpiring under their leadership and are greatly frustrated in their efforts to serve God and His people."[3] He adds, "We learned that they are one of the **most frustrated** occupational groups in our country" (emphasis added). Furthermore, he finds that "the data have shown that many pastors feel overwhelmed by the demands of the job."[4]

Economic Stress

Economic factors can also be a source of stress. Again, research documents this fact. Research studies show that socioeconomic status dramatically impacts life expectancy.[5] Health problems such as high blood pressure, coronary artery disease, obesity, preterm labor, tuberculosis, and cancer increase in low socioeconomic settings.[6]

Why is socioeconomic status important when discussing health risks and the minister? A recent survey showed that pastors face major financial challenges.[7] Some churches treat pastors as if there is holiness in poverty. The issue of economic stress is another aspect of the ministry that predisposes some pastors to ill health and disease.

Our Decaying Bodies

It is a natural part of being human that we have decaying bodies. It is one of the most profound consequences from the fall of Adam. Even when we do not misuse our bodies, they still demonstrate the effects of stress.

Like it or not, your body ages. The process of aging, which remains an enigma to the scientific community to this day, occurs relentlessly in the best of circumstances. In fact, cell death began in the tissues of our bodies *while we were still in our mother's womb.* We were beginning to die before we were even born! Throughout life, decay and aging continue. However, how we care for our bodies dramatically impacts the pace at which the aging process occurs.

There is a widespread misconception that if something is serious enough to cause physical damage, a person will feel it.

This is untrue. The impact of stress from common, daily activities on our mental and physical functions is *not* usually apparent to us. Furthermore, mistreatment of the body creates physical damage *whether we feel it or not!* You won't feel it when stress decreases your white blood cell count. Many such abnormalities will occur before your body's warning signals bring the problem to your attention. By that time, the damage is done. No longer preventable, it *may* be correctable. This is why we rely on our all-knowing Creator to guide our decisions, rather than allowing our own ignorance to destroy our bodies and minds.

> **Mistreatment of the body creates physical damage whether we feel it or not!**

The Physical Impact of Stress

Another way to look at the effects of stress is to study what happens with injury. When you take a serious fall, pain is the body's town crier. Depending on the injury, you may be able to tolerate the pain, but you certainly cannot ignore it.

Pain is an important part of the body's defense mechanism. Remember when your toddler had to learn on his or her own what "hot" meant? No matter how many times you told the child not to, he or she had to touch the oven door. But it only happens once. Sensory memory reminds the little one next time that "hot" and "hurt" are very closely related. Growing up, children learn to apply this information to prevent pain from hot objects.

> **Some emotional stresses cause more physiological abnormalities than physical injury!**

It would be easy if we could *feel* an immediate negative signal when stress occurs. It would encourage us to prevent the stress-causing situation in the future. Unfortunately, the apparent consequences of life stress are very different from those caused by physical injury. They are not usually as dramatic, obvious, immediate, or painful at the beginning. This leads us to minimize the reality of the impact of stress. Thus, we may believe that the consequences of stress are insignificant. This is far from true. In fact, some emotional stresses cause more physiological abnormalities than physical injury!

No one needs to tell you, pastor, that modern ministry includes significant amounts of stress. In an article "Stress in Clergy Families," author Blanton lists the following as the most significant stresses in the ministry family: unclear role expectations, too little time for family and marital communication, lack of clear boundaries for family privacy, health problems, and relocation.[8] One indicator of the increase of stress within modern ministry is the dramatic rise in the divorce rate among pastoral couples.[9] It's sad but true that when stress rises, relationships suffer.

Invisible Damage

As our understanding of illness and disease advances, we are becoming aware of how the human condition, social interactions, relationships, emotional factors, and stress *directly* impact mental and physical health. In fact, very few diseases are the result of a single cause. Most illness comes from multiple factors related to the environment as well as the mind and body.

These facts lead to an important point. Pastors may not manifest any symptoms of disease or ill health. This may give the *illusion* that there is no problem. They don't sense any need to change lifestyle issues that contribute to stress buildup. Somehow, they feel immune to consequences from an unhealthy lifestyle. **But physical and mental damage is occurring nonetheless!**

The fact that you have not succumbed to a disease does not mean that you should continue to take risks! Doing so is foolish. It is much like the person who points to a 90-year-old smoker in excellent physical condition and concludes that smoking does not damage one's body!

God's understanding is infinite. Ours is minuscule. His ways are always right even when we do not fully understand them. We must not assume that our earthen vessel will defy the natural consequences of an unhealthy lifestyle. Remember, our body is decaying. Our only hope of assuring that this process occurs at the slowest possible rate is following God's plan in every area of our life.

We must not underestimate the dire impact of living a chronically stressful life. No one knows for certain how frequently a pastor experiences medical complications as a result of the pastoral lifestyle. However, research certainly weights the possibility in favor of it being true. What is the problem here? Does God call this large group of people into health risks? Or do the personal decisions and lifestyle patterns predispose ministers to ill health and disease?

It is obvious that no one can remove *all* stress from life. However, it is possible to apply God's plan for preventing and relieving stress so that it does not build up in ways that set off the time bomb.

Instead of simply lowering health-care costs for pastors, we need to find ways to prevent ill health and disease in the first place.

Newspapers and magazines regularly run stories about health-care costs and its crisis. Many articles offer ideas for health-care revisions to lower costs. Instead of simply lowering health-care costs for pastors, we need to find ways to prevent ill health and disease in the first place.

Perhaps by now you have heard so many "inescapable" complications inherent to the pastoral lifestyle that you believe these serious health risks are just a part of "bearing your cross." This is not true. Our Creator offers a health protection plan. It is a plan that protects health and prevents unnecessary ill health and disease, especially from stress buildup. At this time in our society's history, we need Christian leaders who will show us **God's health plan** by being obedient to it as revealed in the Word.

That's a major theme of this book: understanding God's perspective and prescription concerning health. If anything in the preceding chapters has made you reevaluate your work schedule, priorities, or stress level, keep reading. There are more answers to come.

WHAT ABOUT YOU?

- Did you realize how health-care statistics for ministers identify them as a high-risk group for ill health and disease?

- Do you recognize places in your normal work routine where stress factors exist?

- Have you believed the myth that if stress were severe enough to cause damage, you would be able to identify symptoms of a problem?

- Do you feel lack of control over your workload or its pace?

- Do economic factors add stress to your life?

- Are you ready to discover some key answers from God's Word?

ENDNOTES

1. Today, district insurance plans replace this nationwide denominational plan. Since it still links pastors as a group, it still ranks them in a higher premium group.

2. J. Siegrist, D. Klein, and H. Matschinger, "Occupational Stress, Coronary Risk Factors, and Cardiovascular Responsiveness," in H. Weiner, D. Hellhammer, I. Florin, et al., eds., *Frontiers of Stress Research* (Toronto: Hans Huber, 1989), 323-35.

3. George Barna, *Today's Pastors* (Ventura, Calif.: Regal Books, 1993), 24.

4. Ibid., 59.

5. G. W. Brown and T. Harris, *Social Origins of Depression* (London: Tavistock Press, 1978).

6. S. L. Syme and L. F. Berkman, "Social Class, Susceptibility, and Sickness," *Am J Epidemiol* 104 (1976): 1-8.

7. Barna, *Today's Pastors*, 37-40.

8. P. W. Blanton, "Stress in Clergy Families: Managing Work and Family Demands," *Family Process* 26 (1992): 315-30.

9. R. Goodling and C. Smith, "Clergy Divorce: A Survey of Issues and Emerging Ecclesiastical Structures," *J Pastoral Care* 37 (1983): 277-91.

CHAPTER 10

Health from God's Perspective

Today's world emphasizes healthy living in a way no other age has headlined it. Fitness club memberships are on the rise. Every neighborhood has at least one runner you can almost set your watch by. Natural foods, organic foods, fat-free foods fill the shelves of grocery stores and cupboards. However, the emphasis on healthy living does not equal a healthy society.

Unfortunately I have found that Christians emphasize the spiritual to the near exclusion of the physical. Perhaps it is a reaction to living in a world that has emphasized the physical and excluded the spiritual. God does not draw such lines.

No Separation

God does not separate the spiritual, mental, and physical aspects of human life. When He created man, He created him with these dimensions in seamless unity. The Bible reveals that God understands us as a whole: spirit, soul, and body (1 Thess. 5:23).

Thinking we can artificially separate these human aspects has been a problem in society, medicine, and even Christianity. For example, the philosophy of gnosticism ultimately failed for this reason. Gnostics believed that the "flesh" and the "spirit" were totally separate and did not impact each other.

The medical world is taking a new look at the belief that man is more than a sum of his parts. They understand that a person must be treated as a whole even when focusing on a diseased or wounded part of the person. Dr. Herbert Weiner from the UCLA School of Medicine summarized it this way: "Mental and physical health are indivisible: The world of medicine cannot *artificially* be divided into the mental and the physical."[1]

A Misunderstanding

When Christian leaders fail to perceive God's holistic view of man, it generates a misunderstanding. It goes something like this: As long as I work for the Lord, He will protect me from physical problems that would occur if I were pursuing "merely secular" goals. Unfortunately, many pastors believe that God will keep them physically well as long as they are doing "His" work. After all, aren't we supposed to ask for *strength for the day*, our *daily bread*, and *endurance* in the hard times? Can't we count on God to *get us through* until He confirms that our work is finished? Of course we can, but it is only half the truth. It leaves a misconception that has prematurely ended the ministry of many Christian leaders at a time when God wanted them to reap their greatest harvest.

> The misunderstanding: As long as I work for the Lord, He will protect me from physical problems that would occur if I were pursuing "secular" goals.

A Good Place to Start

Let me restate one of the basic premises of this book: Ministry-related stress directly impacts the physical, mental, and spiritual health of a person. The reverse is also true. That is, physical and mental health problems directly affect a person's ministry. This dispels the myth that we can mistreat our bodies without impacting our spiritual lives (1 Cor. 3:16-17). No matter how "spiritual" or important the activity is, overinvolvement will eventually do the same physical damage to the Christian as it will to the non-Christian. It will bring about the same ill health or disease for the pastor as for the layman. It is error to believe otherwise.

Health and God's Laws

Many people act as if there is no connection between good health habits and a person's spiritual life. However, the Bible clearly shows a link between the two. For example, a substantial portion of Levitical law had to do with health issues. Analyzing these laws from a medical perspective reveals that Leviticus was a sophisticated public health document. Actually, this should not surprise us. Long before humans had any knowledge about infectious disease principles or contagious microscopic agents, God fully understood health, disease, and the human body. That's why we need to obey His health-related commands even when we do not understand them.

It is easy to look at the ancient Hebrew culture and consider them ignorant regarding health issues as compared to our sophisticated knowledge and advanced technology. This simply is not true. In fact, our current understanding of health and disease remains quite minuscule, given the complexity of the human body. In my medical research, I repeatedly discover that *the actual* cause of most diseases remains *entirely unknown*. Because of this, it is important for us to trust the plan God lays out for us in Scripture. Our minute understanding of how the human body works is no match for the knowledge and insight of the One who created us. He continues to control every physiological process, including the ones we do not understand.

New Understandings About Stress

What medical science has been uncovering about stress only exposes God's genius. New findings in the neurobiology and physiology of stress reveal the role of *neurotransmitters* and stress hormones in the genesis of disease. The research uncovers an intricate and complex interaction between health and life circumstances. Part of the role of the *neuroendocrine* system involves monitoring and controlling these interactions in every organ of the body. Scientific investigation of this system clearly reveals that physical and emotional responses to stressful experience play a **major** role in the development of disease.

In earlier chapters, especially chapter 2, we looked closely at this interaction by identifying the stress connection to disorders affecting the cardiovascular as well as the digestive system. It should surprise no one that the recent findings about this stress connection only reveal the wisdom behind God's plan for health. Millennia before scientists coined the term "neurotransmitter," God created a process by which stress activates certain hormones that send messages to organs. These messages, if repeated too often, cause damage. We are just beginning to glimpse the true genius of the Ancient of Days who knew us before we were conceived (Ps. 139). We cannot separate the physical and spiritual aspects of human life. God, in His infinite wisdom, views us as a whole: spirit, soul, and body.

Attempting to carry out God's work apart from God's plan is not God's will!

Paying attention to this truth means paying attention to God's command to rest. It means obeying the Sabbath cycle. It means protecting your body and mind from overload. While many aspects of the modern pastoral lifestyle place ministers at high risk for disease and ill health, God wants to protect them with restorative rest. Never forget that attempting to carry out **God's work** apart from **God's plan** is not **God's will!**

What Moses Learned

There is a biblical story that masterfully outlines the practical benefit of following God's plan for insuring that His leaders are able to rest. Consider it God's prescription for the too-busy pastor.

The public ministry of Moses began at a frantic pace with a whirlwind of historic events: standing before Pharaoh, the plagues, the Passover, the Red Sea, striking the rock at Rephidim, the war with the Amalekites. Can you imagine being the leader of hundreds of thousands of God's people during such incredible times? What an enormous weight of responsibility Moses must have felt.

After these events, Moses' father-in-law, Jethro, came to him. Jethro had seen something that really bothered him. He observed that Moses would "judge the people" all day long "from the morning until the evening." Then, "when Moses' father-in-law saw all that he was doing for the people, he said, 'What is this thing that you are doing for the people? Why do you *alone* sit as judge and all the people stand about you from morning until evening?'" (Exod. 18:13-14, emphasis added).

Moses responded to his father-in-law, "Because the people come to me to inquire of God. When they have a dispute, it comes to me, and I judge between a man and his neighbor, and make known the statutes of God and His laws" (vv. 15-16).

You Will Surely Wear Out

At this point, Jethro counsels Moses with keen insight from God: "The thing that you are doing is not good. *You will surely wear out,* both yourself and these people who are with you, *for the task is too heavy for you;* you cannot do it alone" (vv. 17-18, emphases added).

The words are clear and direct. And the words not only were for Moses but also reverberate through the centuries to all whom God has called to lead His people. Listen to them one more time: **"The thing that you are doing is not good. You will surely wear out . . . for the task is too heavy for you"**!

Fortunately, Jethro did not communicate his message as a critic, telling Moses that he was doing something wrong. This father-in-law spoke from compassion and love. He offered Moses a plan, not another problem. "Now listen to me: I shall give you counsel, and God be with you. You be the people's representative before God, and you bring the disputes to God, then teach them the statutes and the laws, and make known to them the way in which they are to walk, and the work they are to do" (vv. 19-20).

Does This Sound Familiar?

Can you believe it? This is *exactly* the same plan that the apostles organized when the dispute about feeding the widows broke out in Acts 6 (vv. 1-7). What did the apostles tell the people? "We will devote ourselves to prayer, and to the ministry of the word" (v. 4). Didn't Jethro tell Moses to do the same thing? "Teach them the statutes and the laws" (Exod. 18:20). This is a good example showing unity between the Old and New Testaments. In fact, every important spiritual truth is found in both Testaments. That's why finding this mandate in both places reminds God's servant that a preacher of the Word must reject anything that displaces God's clear priority. Doing so *"is not good"* (v. 17). Why? Because *"the task is too heavy . . . You will surely wear out"* (v. 18).

Look again at Jethro's counsel. First, he identified the problem. He declared that Moses was working the wrong way. Next, he identified the consequence. "You will surely wear out." Instead of leaving Moses with what *not* to do, Jethro told him what he *should* do. Moses *should* teach God's laws and precepts to the people. He *should* instruct them how to apply God's commands. He *should* make it his priority over any other ministry detail, but he *should not* wear himself out.

Delegate

Jethro wasn't finished with his counsel. God helped Jethro to review Moses' leadership priority, but he also reviewed the people's responsibilities. He went on to say: "Furthermore, you shall select out of all the people able men who fear God, men of truth, those who hate dishonest gain; and you shall place these over them, as leaders of thousands, of hundreds, of fifties and of tens. And let them judge the people at all times; and let it be that every major dispute they will bring to you, but every minor dispute they themselves will judge. So it will be easier for you, *and they will bear the burden with you*" (Exod. 18:21-22, emphasis added).

Again, we hear the counsel echoed in Act 6:3: appoint "men of good reputation, full of the Spirit and of wisdom" to oversee serving the tables. Even the qualifications are similar to the list in Acts. Jethro lists the following as important leadership traits: able, God-fearing, truthful, with an honest work ethic. The Acts list calls for appointed leaders to be of good reputation, Spirit-filled, wise and able to lead.

In both stories, God did not minimize the importance of serving tables or helping people. He simply made it clear that if the leaders took too many responsibilities upon themselves, the task would be too heavy, and they would wear out. Instead, He gave Moses high-quality ministry partners who could bear the burden with him.

Able to Endure

As clear and direct as this teaching is, the full counsel does not end at Exod. 18:22. In the very next sentence, the scripture clearly shows that obedience to God's Word about delegation directly connects to endurance. Immediately after Jethro told Moses to appoint leaders to help him bear the burden, his very next words were: "If you do this thing and God so commands you, then you will be *able to endure,* and all these people also will go to their place in peace" (v. 23, emphasis added). Notice again the very clear inference: *"If* you do this thing . . . *then* you will be able to endure" (emphases added)!

> Scripture clearly shows that obedience to God's Word about delegation directly connects to endurance.

It is indisputable that the leader of God's people has been called to pray and preach the Word. While this calling identifies what the minister is *to do,* it also identifies what the leader is *not to do.* God's leader is to relinquish anything that makes it difficult to do the primary work He ordains. It is essential that today's Christian leaders stop clinging to ministry activities that prevent fulfilling God's primary call. Scripture is clear. If leaders do not lessen their loads, they will not endure. Their ministries and their lives will be shortened!

There is one more aspect of this story that is important. Moses' leadership career was 40 years long. God gave Moses this lesson in delegation near the beginning of his ministry. It came within three months after the Exodus from Egypt (Exod. 19:1). Moses was on a self-destructive road. He was trying to be all things to all people. He was trying to be prophet, arbitrator, judge, lawyer, and marriage counselor all in one. God knew he couldn't do it. Jethro knew he couldn't do it. And Moses was learning he couldn't do it. However, Moses welcomed a way to maintain ministry without overloading himself. He appointed the leaders and delegated responsibilities from the beginning, and he *was enabled* to endure.

It is a clear biblical pattern for God-called leaders. Learn to delegate at the *beginning* of ministry. Follow the model of Moses and the apostles, who delegated certain ministry responsibilities in order to focus on prayer and preaching. Whether you are at the beginning of your ministry or not, you can **begin** to obey God's will and His purpose today. For the sake of your body, your mind, your family, your church, and especially the Kingdom, do not neglect this aspect of establishing a healthy lifestyle.

Another Model

Another ministry model demonstrates the inescapable wisdom for developing a lifestyle pattern that includes rest. Who handled more ministry pressure than Jesus did? His ministry was in full swing. He had preached in Nazareth, cast out demons, and performed miraculous healings. Simple fishermen declared Him the Son of God and left full boats of fresh fish to follow this new-styled Fisherman. Even the demons knew He was the Son of God. Crowds followed Him wherever He went. People wouldn't leave Him alone. The impact of His ministry had been so awesome that He asked some of His followers not to report the miracles. Despite this apparent attempt to slow the growth of His fame, the Scripture tells us that "the news about Him was spreading even farther, and great multitudes were gathering to hear Him and to be healed of their sicknesses" (Luke 5:15).

Try to imagine what it must have been like. Here was Jesus, performing miracles that the world had never seen. Before His baptism, John had exclaimed that he was "not [even] fit to untie the thong of [Jesus'] sandals" (3:16). Simon Peter, enamored by His presence, fell down and said, "Depart from me, for I am a sinful man, O Lord!" (5:8). Despite these great testimonies, Jesus understood a call upon His life that was far beyond anything His contemporaries could verbalize. It is clear that Jesus understood himself to be the One whom the mighty prophets of Israel had foretold. Jesus knew that He was the One who would one day sit on King David's throne (Isa. 9:7). Jesus fully understood His call and His mission to the world.

In Luke 5:15, Jesus finds himself in the midst of great multitudes of desperate people with enormous needs. In this situation, we see an amazing turn of events. One can scarcely find two consecutive verses that, from human perspective, seem so far apart. Verse 15 ends with the phrase "and great multitudes were gathering to hear Him and to be healed of their sicknesses." The next statement by Luke seems out of place and totally unexpected: "He Himself would *often* slip away to the wilderness and pray" (v. 16, emphasis added).

A Strange Priority

How could the One who had been sent to save the world justify leaving these people to go to the wilderness by himself? He only had three and a half years to set in motion the events that would enable His Church to take the message of salvation to all humankind. Each day—indeed, each moment was of infinite worth to humanity! Only Jesus could give them what they needed. How could Jesus "waste" precious time isolating himself from the needs of a desperate, dying world?

How could Jesus "waste" precious time isolating himself from the needs of a desperate, dying world?

Some might say that Jesus was setting an example for His followers to emphasize the importance of prayer in their lives.

Of course this is true, but I believe that it was not the *primary* purpose.

There were many things that Jesus did to leave an example for His disciples. He washed His disciples' feet to model servanthood. He changed the Passover meal to incorporate the new covenant. He laid down His life. If this retreat was for modeling only, Jesus could have stated its importance, demonstrated it, and moved on to another lesson. That's not what He did with this lesson. He repeated it often.

A Necessity

The reason Jesus often took time away to rest and pray was because He could not fulfill His calling unless He did. No other compulsion makes sense. Jesus did everything from His motivation to save the world. Jesus knew that He must go often to His Father to rest and restore His weary heart, mind, and body. Although Jesus was fully divine, He was also fully human! Though He remained sinless, Jesus experienced the finiteness, frailty, and limitations of His humanity (Heb. 4:15). Thus, it was absolutely necessary that He find rest and strength in frequent wilderness experiences with His Father.

No one questions that Jesus had a heart of compassion. He would not have left needy multitudes unless it was mandatory to do so. The fact that He often did implies that His very ability to carry out the saving of the world depended on His time in the wilderness.

If Jesus could not effectively minister to the world without His time of rest and prayer, how can we expect to? Satan knows that if he can get us working in our own strength, he has already defeated our ministry at its very foundation. Thus, he seeks to cut off our Source of power. In fact, if we never do anything more for the Kingdom than what we can accomplish by ourselves, the world is in trouble. Even if our ministry comes from good intentions and legitimate motives, anything done apart from the Holy Spirit's leadership and enabling is not from faith **or from God** (John 15:4-5)!

This has profound implications for today's pastor. It exposes the fallacy of thinking that you can't afford to leave ministry tasks without the church collapsing in your absence. It reminds all leaders that to do God's work God's way must involve balancing work and rest in the same way that Jesus did.

Following Jesus

Most people who commit time to ministry do so out of a desire to serve and obey their Heavenly Father. However, this good motive can be misdirected. For instance, a committed pastor can find more reasons to skip a weekly day of rest than the children of Israel concocted when they robbed the land of its Sabbaths. Busy Christian leaders point to their heavy burdens for the world around them. They highlight the enormity of the suffering and pain that compels their diligent service.

> **Nothing justifies disobedience to God.**

The needs are endless! However, this is where the life of Jesus challenges us to work differently from the world. Nothing justifies disobedience to God. Not church awards. Not new buildings. Not even growing attendance records, as good and important as they are. God's command and Jesus' model of rest in the midst of pressured ministry is unavoidable. As ministers and servants of the One who called you, you must follow Jesus' model of finding peace and being *at peace* in the middle of a frantic pace, even when there is pressure to do otherwise.

Your Response

I realize that people surround you with their needs and their suffering. Often it is desperation that defies description. In fact, you may feel guilty taking the time to read this book while there are so many things of eternal significance waiting. Your ministry task list swells every day. Too many times it seems that no one else will do the work. The weight of carrying out God's eternal plan in your church or community may feel as if it rests on your shoulders alone. To a pastor under this kind of ministry pressure, the message of Jesus is a paradox. **Go to the wilderness. Go often!** As important as your ministry is, as significant as your vision for God's work has become, as urgent as your calling burns within, that's how important, significant, and urgent His call to you is: **Go to the wilderness. Go often!**

The Messiah who desires to use you to rescue His world cannot use exhausted servants. He cannot fulfill His eternal plan with tired workers. He cannot fight the battle between good and evil with weary warriors. Therefore, just as the Lord showed us in the midst of the most important ministry of all time, you must leave the needy multitudes to go to the wilderness. Away from your office. Away from the phone in your home or your car. Make it a habit to do it *often*, just like Jesus. Who knows what kind of time bomb you may be preventing. Or who you may be able to help because your ministry endured.

> The Messiah who desires to use you to rescue His world cannot use exhausted servants.

WHAT ABOUT YOU?

- **Do you treat the spiritual aspects of your ministry as if there are no physical implications from stress and overwork?**

- **Do you count on God to protect you physically even when you do not obey His instructions involving the balance between work and rest?**

- **Are you wearing yourself out because you cling to too many ministry details that should be delegated?**

- **Do you understand that your ability to endure directly relates to your obedience to God's instruction concerning effective ministry?**

- **Do you follow Jesus' model and plan "wilderness" experiences to restore your body, mind, and soul?**

- Did you take your day off last week? Will you plan to take it this week?

ENDNOTES

1. Herbert Weiner, *Perturbing the Organism: The Biology of Stressful Experience* (Chicago: University of Chicago Press, 1992), 51.

CHAPTER 11

Realigning Your Ministry Perspective

My wife and I have always been very active in a local church. She has served as children's ministries director in three churches and has directed children's choirs for 17 years. I have served in local church leadership positions, taught Sunday School, and participated in music ministry. The church has always been an important part of our lives. We really care about the Body of Christ. However, the Lord reminded me *again* of a timeless principle in the not-too-distant past.

The church that we were attending experienced rapid growth in the previous five years. Morning worship increased from 110 to 350. Great things were happening in the congregation. In the middle of this growth, our pastor moved to another church. While we trusted God's leadership in this change, we found ourselves in the midst of a pastoral interim. The church leadership began the prescribed process to call a new pastor. In the denomination I belong to, elected church leadership meet with the district superintendent to seek God's direction in calling a new pastor to the church. To begin the process, we met to pray together and make a list of possible candidates.

Just as the process reached the final decision-making stage, the Lord taught me something that I hope I never forget. To say that I was interested in the outcome is an understatement. We were looking for the spiritual leader who would take our church to the next step of individual and corporate growth. I believed that I had important input to give to the process. However, when it came to the last two meetings, I had to be out of town to keep previously scheduled speaking commitments.

I will never forget sitting in the hotel room in Tampa, Florida, on a Monday afternoon, lamenting the fact that I would not be a part of that final moment when we agreed upon a name. In a way that God has done few times in my life, He spoke with unmistakable clarity. The message was profound but simple. The Lord reminded me that *He* was capable of calling a pastor for *His* church. Immediately, my shoulders relaxed. They no longer carried the responsibility of this very important decision. What a relief to understand that *God can take care of His Church!*

I realize that I am not the only person who has forgotten these truths. In fact, one of the major factors contributing to exhausted, burned-out Christian leaders is a failure to grasp the implications of the truth that *the Church is not ours!* I'm sure that you have preached the truth that *the Church belongs to God.* However; it's one thing to talk about this truth; it's quite another to live it.

Perhaps part of the difficulty lies in the fact that the Church is not simply another human organization. On the surface there are similarities. There are structure and process that people administrate. There is a purpose and mission by which the organization evaluates itself. There is a budget and the need for financial accountability and reporting. However, the Church is not just a sum of its people and processes. The Church is the Body of Christ. It is the tangibility of our resurrected Lord on earth. I don't believe any pastor purposefully forgets this fact; however, I do believe that misunderstanding the implications of this truth is one of the most basic causes for exhaustion among them.

Not a Human Organization

We live in a world of human organizations. Every institution from the smallest business to the largest government has an organizational structure. The success of the organization depends primarily upon the quality of leadership and how diligently the individuals within the organization do their jobs. When a local church takes people who work in human organizations and welcomes them into the Body, they bring more than their skills and cooperation. They bring their ideas about how an organization should work. Since, at least superficially, the institutional church appears to function just like other human institutions, they naturally transplant successful business philosophies and methods.

The institution of the church, apart from the direct, personal power of Christ, is no more able to save the souls of men than the National Football League or Kiwanis Club.

Some of these principles effectively make the transfer to the church. However, since the foundation of the Church is supernatural, not all business principles apply to its supernatural nature. By the mysterious and awesome power of the Holy Spirit, the Church is the Body of Christ on earth.

Confusion regarding this issue leads to numerous problems. First, it is possible to substitute membership in a human institution (*a local church*) for membership in the Body of Christ (*the* Church). Scripture teaches that, tragically, some people who have "called upon the name of the Lord" will be told that He never knew them (Matt. 7:22-23; 25:1-13). Jesus directed this prophecy toward those who substituted a human institution for the true Church. However, *the institution of the church, apart from the direct, personal power of Christ, is no more able to save the souls of men than the National Football League or Kiwanis Club.*

The second problem is a great albatross for church leaders. That is, many people treat their commitment to the church in the same way they treat commitments to any other human institution including job and community and social organizations. This attitude distresses many church leaders. Pastors are trying to build God's Church with people who are more committed to city league basketball.

Allow me to describe a strange paradox. I believe that I am

writing to some who have made the same *theological* error. Unlike the others whom I have described, you *are very* committed to the work of ministry. In fact, you are spending enormous amounts of time, energy, and emotion trying to build a church because you understand its eternal significance. However, if you really believe the Church to be more than a human institution, you must demonstrate it with more than human energy and strategies. Human strategies produce human results. Matt. 7:24-27 calls such endeavors sinking sand.

Corporate CEO philosophy has the tendency to replace the Cornerstone with a human leader.

Let me illustrate. The pastor is not the CEO of the church. To adopt that philosophy is to undermine the truth that Jesus is the Cornerstone of His Church. Corporate CEO philosophy has the tendency to replace the Cornerstone with a human leader because the strategy comes from a human organization. The Scripture is very clear here: No one but Christ himself functions as the Church's Cornerstone.

It is possible to build a "great" church and make it appear that Christ is the Cornerstone, only to find the church in collapse when a pastor leaves. It is possible to build a successful human institution without building the *true* Body of Christ. However, such a possibility is great tragedy.

All church leaders must *continually* reevaluate whether they work to build God's Church by their own strength or by the enabling power of Christ. Anyone who does not build on *The Cornerstone* builds in vain (Eph. 2:19-22; Luke 20:17-18). Furthermore, any church built by *human* strength will have little more eternal impact than any other human institution! First Cor. 3:10-15 reminds us that the fruits of such labor will burn in the end.

Substituting Human Strategies

Another cause for misplaced energy occurs when church leaders incorporate management techniques from the secular world. Don't get me wrong. I understand that there are legitimate ideas from the world of business that offer valuable help to the local church.

However, successful institutional growth can *mimic* growth of Christ's Body when human wisdom, strength, and management style build it. Real growth as Jesus defines it is when Christ's saving work adds people to His Body. Successful church growth may involve numbers at the beginning, but it does not end with numbers.

Successful institutional growth can mimic growth of Christ's Body when human wisdom, strength, and management style build it.

Success to the Body of Christ means that Christ continues to change lives and fill them with His Holy Spirit. To consider anything else Christ-pleasing growth is to be satisfied with the wrong definition of success.

Serious problems surface when Christian leaders fail to understand that Christ *will build His Church* (Matt. 16:18). God never intended His Church to function as another human institution. He wants it to bear the unmistakable marks that set it apart from any other human organization. He wants to use us as His building tools. However, we can only be a part of what Christ is doing to build *His* Church when we work by *His* power.

The Gates of Hell Notwithstanding

There is another important issue that Christ's words in Matt. 16 reveal. After promising to build His Church, He also announces that "the gates of Hades shall not overpower it" (v. 18). Either this is true or it is not. If it is true, and I believe it is, then it leads us to a very uncomfortable conclusion about some ministries today. While Satan looks to attack any person or process where God is working, Jesus has made it clear that Satan will not be able to overpower God's work. Then what does it mean when everything points to the possibility that Satan is winning? A ministry crumbles. A church divides. A church leader falls. Church leadership, clergy and laity, must ask serious questions about whose church they are building. Is it possible that if the forces of evil seem to render your service for the Master ineffective, maybe you aren't doing the service that He wants you to do?

Christ did not call anyone to *easy* work in His kingdom. He promised that obedience ultimately brings about His purposes. However, it must be *His* ministry, *His* purpose, and *His* methods. But even in this case, not all *effective* ministries will be *successful*. If they were, most of the world would already have accepted the gospel. When Jesus told the parable of the soils, He taught that not all ground is fertile (Matt. 13:1-9, 18-23). The problem is, we cannot correctly identify fertile ground apart from His direct, continuous, and specific leading. That's the point! *We can dedicate our lives to a ministry that has no chance of succeeding.* With exceptional talent and commendable energy, we will accomplish very little of *eternal* value unless we are continually led by the Father (John 15:5).

> **We can dedicate our lives to a ministry that has no chance of succeeding.**

The Problem with Human Plans

Are you holding on tightly to *your* plan to build your church? It won't work! Instead it can lead to exhaustion, health problems, mental disorders, disillusionment, and perhaps even to bitterness toward God. In fact, it may already have.

Much of the weariness that Christian leaders experience shows that leaders try to build God's Church through overwork. Don't misunderstand. God calls us to diligent service (2 Tim. 4:6-7; Heb. 10:36). He understands that His call requires hard work. The problem is that His mission to save the world is far beyond our talents and strengths. When we carry the work on our shoulders, the work is doomed to fail from the beginning.

His Church, Not Mine!

The whole thrust of the new covenant is that Jesus came to save the world by *His* plan, *His* blood, *His* wisdom, *His* strength, and *His* authority. The *entire* responsibility for building *His* Church belongs to His Holy Spirit. In one sense, we share this Kingdom-building responsibility with the Holy Spirit. However, weary, burned-out church leaders can no longer carry their share of the load. Let's face it, if God has to use tired, burned-out people to save the whole world, the world is in big trouble. *It is time to give the Church back to the Master!* Each leader must testify to His sovereignty with words *and* action. Each minister must recognize and reaffirm that it is *His* Church, not mine.

An Urgent Ministry

If ever anyone experienced God's call to perform a ministry of incredible urgency, it was Paul. It began with a call so dramatic that it literally blinded him to everything else. That Damascus road experience proved unforgettable in Paul's life. It formed the foundation for a level of drive and focus that has few equals in Christian history.

So Little Time

God has always had a heart to save the *whole* world (John 3:16-17). Paul understood this and may have faced one of the most overwhelming ministry tasks in the history of the Church. In Paul's time, the ratio between Gentiles and Jews numbered 1,000 to 1.[1] It is difficult to imagine the urgency Paul experienced as he followed God's call to preach the gospel. He knew that the entire Gentile world remained in darkness. It was enough to push him to a frantic pace. But it didn't. Paul did not allow his intense desire to preach the Good News to derail him from his higher calling to remain totally obedient to Christ.

Hurry Up and Wait

Amazingly, God delayed Paul's ministry for over a decade! Paul lived the first three years of this time out in the middle of nowhere. God sent him to Arabia, a bleak, lifeless, forsaken desert (Gal. 1:15-18).

Before we go on, let's identify how surprising this delay was. Paul wrote at least 13 books of the New Testament. During his missionary journeys, he preached to the entire known world. It is difficult to overstate the impact of Paul's letters and missionary endeavors on the history of the Christian Church. One biblical scholar put it this way: "From this point of the apostolic history, Paul appears as the great figure of *every* event" (emphasis added).[2]

So why did God want Paul to *waste* three years in the Arabian Desert? From our perspective, Paul answered his call with all the tools necessary from the beginning: He was born again, was Spirit-filled (three days later), knew the Scripture backward and forward, and was zealous with unparalleled commitment. Why did the Lord send him to the wilderness to do "nothing"? This shows where man's wisdom and God's wisdom part ways (Gal. 1:15).

No Shortcuts

How many people died without hearing the gospel before God released Paul from the wilderness? Wasn't that a good enough reason to begin immediately? Evidently not. God knew that there were some things Paul needed to learn that he could *only* learn in the wilderness. He knew that if Paul began his ministry too early, some would come to salvation in the short run, but many would be prevented from hearing the gospel in the long run. Paul laid aside an intense desire to set out immediately on *his own* journey because he knew that the wisdom of man is foolishness to God (1 Cor. 1:20-29).

How Paul must have wanted to take a shortcut. Instead he seemed to understand that bypassing God's plan would have devastating results, *even when following that plan made no sense from a human perspective.*

There is another aspect of God's call to Paul that we should not miss. The years of preparation enabled him to withstand intense pressures that he would face in the years to come. It prepared him to surface as a leader among the apostles. It matured his leadership style, focused his priorities, and deepened his relationship with Christ. How do we know this? Acts 13:1 lists several prophets and teachers, beginning with Barnabas and ending with Saul. It records the first missionary journey that began with Saul of Tarsus leaving Antioch for Cyprus (vv. 1-4). Something happened on this island that was to change this new follower and the rest of the world. As Saul testified before the Roman governor, Sergius Paulus, a false prophet attempted to divert the governor from listening to this missionary's message. When Saul confronted the local "sorcerer" (vv. 6, 8, KJV) and pronounced him spiritually and physically blind, Sergius Paulus saw what happened and believed (v. 12). After that, Saul's name change occurred, and he became the leader of the delegation (vv. 9, 13). How did this change occur?

Saul Becomes Paul

The name Saul goes back to the first king of Israel who came from the tribe of Benjamin, the same tribe that New Testament Saul shared (1 Sam. 9:1-2; Phil. 3:5). Saul of the Old Testament was a man of great stature: "a choice and handsome man, and there was not a more handsome person than he among the sons of Israel; from his shoulders and up he was taller than any of the people" (1 Sam. 9:2). But all of King Saul's superlative attributes by themselves did not win a place for him in God's plans. Unfortunately, Saul "the Great" was a self-centered man, intent on his own self-aggrandizement. To King Saul, *his* ideas made more sense than the *foolish* plans that God had for Israel (chap. 15).

Although Paul did not have the physical stature of his predecessor (2 Cor. 10:10), he was unsurpassed among the Hebrews in religious matters. In Philippians chapter 3, he says these things about himself: "Although I myself might have confidence even in the flesh. If anyone else has a mind to put confidence in the flesh, I far more: circumcised the eighth day, of the nation of Israel, of the tribe of Benjamin, a Hebrew of Hebrews; as to the Law, a Pharisee; as to zeal, a persecutor of the church; as to the righteousness which is in the Law, found blameless" (vv. 4-6).

According to Jewish tradition, Saul of Tarsus was a *great man!*

Go back to Acts 13. Until this point Scripture refers to this converted Jew as Saul. For the first time in verse 9, Luke calls him Paul. As Luke penned this name, he was really writing the Greek name Paulos. The Greek reader understood that this name meant "little," "small," or "tiny." Saul the Great, the one whose accolades superseded his contemporaries, had become Paul, the little.

In the midst of this "demotion," there is paradoxical change. Saul, who had been at the bottom of the list of teachers and prophets (v. 1), surfaces as the leader. In fact, immediately after the name change, the names of his peers *were no longer even mentioned!* Instead Scripture speaks of "Paul and his companions" (v. 13). It was an announcement that Paul would lead the ministry to the Gentile world. God could not use Saul of Tarsus to carry out His mighty plan until the *great man* became Paulos—the *little, small, tiny, insignificant man.*

Wisdom from the Wilderness

Perhaps now we can understand why God wanted Paul to spend many years preparing for his historic ministry. Contrary to what many would expect, God was not making Saul of Tarsus into a great man. Rather, *He was making a great man into a humble servant!* This makes no sense to us. Not only was God *wasting* the world's time by making Paul spend many long years in training, but He was also removing what he had depended on for greatness before. He was teaching him that what had made him a great man before belonged on a rubbish pile! "But whatever things were gain to me, those things I have counted as loss for the sake of Christ. More than that, I count all things to be loss in view of the surpassing value of knowing Christ Jesus my Lord, for whom I have suffered the loss of all things, and count them but *rubbish* in order that I may gain Christ" (Phil. 3:7-8, emphasis added).

Why did God delay the start of Paul's much-needed ministry? Because God could do His greatest work when Paul considered his greatness as rubbish, his eloquence as gibberish, his talents as worthless, his mind as foolish, his ancestry as meaningless, and his strength as weakness. To be great, he had to take the place of a servant, with childlike dependence on his Master (Matt. 18:1-4; 23:10-12; Luke 22:24-26). When God had performed this work in this man, Paul could testify: "On my own behalf I will not boast, *except in regard to my weaknesses. . . .* And He has said to me, 'My grace is sufficient for you, for power is perfected in weakness.' Most gladly, therefore, I will rather boast about my weaknesses, that the power of Christ may dwell in me. Therefore I am well content with weaknesses, with insults, with distresses, with persecutions, with difficulties, for Christ's sake; *for when I am weak, then I am strong*" (2 Cor. 12:5, 9-10, emphases added).

Where's Your Wilderness?

Has God been trying to send you to an Arabian wilderness? Have you been trying to develop skills so that you can build a great church, so that you can save souls, so that you can preach the gospel eloquently, so that you can be strong? God wants to take "great" ministers and make them little. No Christian leader will be able to do anything great for the Lord without experiencing transformational pain in the wilderness. It is the pain of rejecting all personal strengths, talents, and eloquence. It is the pain of losing "Saul" to become a "Paul." If this hasn't happened to you, then get ready. God has a wilderness for you. It is a time when He takes *your* greatness, *your* gifts, *your* works, *your* heritage, and *your* wisdom to the rubbish pile (Phil. 3:4-10). It is a time when you lose your greatness to demonstrate more accurately *His* greatness.

This is another way that God shows the wis-

> God has a wilderness for you—a time when He takes your greatness, your gifts, your works, your heritage, and your wisdom to the rubbish pile.

dom behind commanding weekly Sabbaths. These cease and desist times are not just for bodily rest. They are times to let your mind and heart lie fallow so that God can help you see that what you thought was wisdom was nothing more than foolishness in His eyes. During the time when you do not strive in what might be a normal frantic pace, God reconstructs your definition of greatness so that it wears obvious marks of humility and servanthood. In times of isolation and total dependence, He transforms *your* strength into a weakness that acknowledges your need of *His* strength. During your Sabbath, He will remind you that He can build His kingdom even in your absence.

> God reconstructs your definition of greatness so that it wears obvious marks of humility and servanthood.

Your church doesn't need you to be a great minister! It needs you to be a *little* follower who shows Jesus Christ to be great *in* you!

Your church doesn't need a brilliant expositor. It needs you to be a humble servant who will allow Christ to speak *His* timeless wisdom *through* you.

Don't be surprised if God plans some *delays* in your ministry. Choose Paul's obedience over King Saul's partial obedience (1 Sam. 15). Follow Paul's pathway, even when it leads you to an isolated wilderness. Learn what it means to become a quiet, peaceful follower of the Master. Let God make you a channel for His supernatural power. If you allow Him to do this, you will prevent many physical problems associated with disease and ill health. You will reduce negative stress factors that threaten to shorten a minister's years. You will protect your health, your family's health, and your church's health.

Urgent but Not Frantic

The call to rest is not simply to protect the health of the minister, however. When God's leader fails to obey His plan for rest, the disobedience leads to another problem that links to failure in the lives of many pastors. It has to do with the difference between an *urgent* heart and a *frantic* heart. Certainly, God plants a sense of urgency in the call He lays on the life of His servant. Urgency emphasizes timeliness and priority. It does not reflect panic. *Human* reflexes, *human* intellect, *human* plans, and a *human* perspective will drive a frantic heart.

A frantic heart always emphasizes the temporal rather than the eternal. It focuses on immediate, short-term needs but blinds the leader to long-term, eternal ones. Invariably it saps human strength to meet the demands, thereby compromising God's plan.

As strange as it sounds, God calls you to reject responding to *some* immediate needs. He wants to show you that He can bring about His purposes without your overwork. This means that you must be willing to leave some needs unmet while you take your day off each week. It also creates the risk that some people could perceive your obedience as a lack of compassion. It means that you may have to sacrifice your own intense desire to help people while you leave to go to the wilderness.

Urgency emphasizes timeliness and priority. It does not reflect panic.

Follow Jesus, Not Urgency

God has placed a holy sense of urgency within you. This urgency leads you to make many sacrifices. You have given your very life to carry out His urgent call. But listen very carefully. Satan would love to turn a God-ordained urgency into a frantic fiasco. The deceiver tempts you to exchange the Master's direction and control for a frantic, uncontrollable drive!

Satan knows that he has already lost the battle for your soul. That's why he would love to distract you with Martha's busyness instead of Mary's calm adoration for the Master. He desires to tear you away from your quiet place at the feet of Jesus (Luke 10:38-42). He loves to overwhelm you with the sheer magnitude of the desperation surrounding you. If Satan can't make you apathetic, he tries to twist your good intentions toward the wrong focus. Don't get me wrong. A frantic heart is much better than a lukewarm one (Rev. 3:16). But the forces of evil will attempt to use any foothold they can find.

You probably think that I don't understand your situation. And it's partly true. I may not fully understand. However, what I do understand is true for all situations, including mine. God does not promise that there will be time to complete everything that presents itself. He does promise that there is always enough time to obey! Perhaps that's my most urgent message for you today. While there is still time, obey His command to rest and go to the wilderness. Don't delay it because of a building project, special services, or some other important plan or event.

Remember that Jesus was Father-centered, not need-centered (chap. 6). Because of that, when the Father said, "Go to the wilderness," Jesus stopped preaching, healing, and ministering, and *He went to the wilderness.*

I have the strong belief that when you stand face-to-face with God, He will not ask you if you did everything you could think of to serve Him. He will not ask you if you preached every sermon that came to your mind. He will not ask you if you met every need that you saw. Instead, He will ask upon whom was your life centered. I pray that you will allow Him to make the changes in your ministry so that when that day comes, you will be able to say: "Through the power of Your Son, Father, I have glorified You on the earth, having accomplished the work that You gave me to do" (see John 17:4). Nothing less and nothing more.

That's why it is so important to begin to practice obedient restfulness immediately! Listen for His word about timing. If He says delay, then wait! And, in the delay, make sure that you allow Him to remove anything that resembles a Saul so that you can become a Paul, a *great man* who became *little*. Then God's power will perfect your weakness and make it strength. Then you will be able to testify, "For this purpose also I labor, striving according to *His power,* which mightily works within me" (Col. 1:29, emphasis added). Then, and only then, will the ticking time bomb become silent.

WHAT ABOUT YOU?

- Do you treat the church as the Body of Christ, submitting all human strategies to His scrutiny?

- Do you reject overwork in favor of God's reasonable service?

- Have you allowed God to change you from a Saul into a Paul?

- Do you hear God's invitation to the wilderness, and do you answer it more immediately than you answer any other invitation?

- Have you exchanged a frantic heart for a restful one?

- Are you ready to make the changes necessary to become Father-centered?

ENDNOTES

1. D. Larsen, *Jews, Gentiles, and the Church* (Grand Rapids: Discovery House Publishers, 1995), 19.

2. R. K. Harrison, Howard F. Vos, C. J. Barber, eds., *The New Unger's Bible Dictionary* (Chicago: Moody Press, 1988), 792.

CHAPTER 12

Defusing the Time Bomb

During the past five years, I have interviewed many pastors. I have asked: "How do you feel about the expectations and demands placed upon you as a pastor? How much control do you feel that you have over your schedule?" Essentially every one of them said that they have a *major* problem protecting time for rest. *None* of them said that their schedules made it easy to comply with God's plan for weekly rest and frequent time away for renewal. However, in order to obey God's command for a long and effective ministry, His leaders must learn how to defuse demanding schedules that tick like time bombs.

Changing longtime habits requires unsettling transitions. The change involves new priorities and processes. These changes may frustrate some parishioners and leave them with unmet expectations. If meaningful changes are made, many will notice.

Change, even when it makes things better, can *feel* all wrong at first.

It is very difficult to make lifestyle changes. It requires discipline, consistency, endurance, and just plain hard work. However, with a genuine desire to change and faith in God, who is the Source of inner peace, anyone can do it!

The first step necessary in defusing the time bomb is a willingness to recognize that a problem exists. As I talked to pastors about their ministry and workload, they freely admitted several things:

- They worked too hard.
- They spent too little time with their family.

- They did not rest enough.
- They stayed exhausted.
- They felt frustrated, and sometimes hopeless, when they tried to make changes.

The pastors also identified some basic issues that are inherent to the modern professional ministry and encourage overwork. The pastors agreed that any strategy that failed to address these basic issues would not be effective. Here are the three basic challenges they described:

The Challenge to Change a Way of Life

Even when they agreed there was a problem, most pastors accepted their patterns of stress, overwork, and exhaustion as a way of life. They had lived this way for so long, it became a difficult habit to break. Living with overwork, if not more comfortable, was at least more "natural" than attempting change.

The Challenge to Change Expectations

Many pastors wanted to begin taking a regular day off each week and get serious about wilderness experiences. However, they feared that their church leadership might not understand or approve. It's not that parishioners *want* to overwork their pastors; they just get used to their availability.

A pastor of a large church told me that nearly all of his people agreed that he worked too hard. They even expressed their concern by saying, "Pastor, you don't have to do *all* of the funerals, *all* of the weddings, or *all* of the calling." In fact, the church leaders agreed that there were many church functions that did not need the pastor's direct involvement. However, their expectation changed when it was a funeral for *their* family, the wedding of *their* child, or *their* need for a pastoral call. They believed someone else could do it if it involved other people. However, when it in-

> In too many members' minds, the church can take care of *others'* needs, but the pastor must respond to *their* needs.

volved *their* need, there was no acceptable substitute for their pastor. In too many members' minds, the church can take care of *others'* needs, but the pastor must respond to *their* needs. Thus, if a pastor decreases the time commitment to the church, he or she will not be as available to as many people on a one-on-one basis. The pastor risks disapproval from church members for "protecting time" at the expense of their need.

The Challenge to Say No

Most Christians seem to believe that saying yes to ministry opportunities is more *spiritual* than saying no. Several pastors expressed the awkwardness they felt when they tried to say no. They felt the need to explain the reasons for the no. It made them feel defensive. Besides, it was easier to say yes! Yes requires no explanations. Yes receives no raised eyebrows. Yes makes people happy. On the other hand, people equate no with indifference, selfishness, insensitivity, unconcern, or laziness.

Pointing Toward Answers

After listening to the problems these pastors voiced, I realized that identifying challenges was not enough. Recognizing an overloaded schedule is only the first step. The next step is to find a plan that effectively resolves the problem. Again, there are several basic issues that a strategy for change must address. See if you agree.

1. Realize that the momentum of the modern church encourages a frantic lifestyle.

No pastor *naturally* falls into a ministry pace that balances work and rest. Balance always takes effort and discipline. Therefore, a strategy for change must address how to minister to the modern society without adopting a secular lifestyle of stress and imbalance.

2. Establish a *specific* plan for change.

I don't want this book to leave pastors *inspired* about the need to change. I want you to finish reading with a ***plan*** for a healthy lifestyle that leads to a long, fulfilling ministry. A plan for change requires that you divide a goal into achievable steps. It involves scheduled deadlines for evaluation. It involves accountability. A desire to change is not enough.

3. Understand that the church is people.

This is fundamental to breaking the cycle of overwork and exhaustion. As noted earlier, the church is simultaneously a human organization and the supernatural Body of Christ on the earth. The two cannot be separated. Because of this, the human organization, no matter how Spirit-filled, has human frailties. Several realities flow from this:

a. To err is human, even when motives are pure. People in the church will make mistakes. They will not always follow through. They will not always act with mature wisdom. Expecting anything else is to set yourself up for disappointment and stress.

b. It is easy to adopt the secular mind-set of our society. Living in a sinful world clouds the understanding of even the most dedicated followers of Christ. Paul testifies with these words: "For we know in part, and we prophesy in part. . . . For now we see in a mirror dimly" (1 Cor. 13:9, 12). You will adopt the philosophies and strategies of the models closest to you. As long as the closest model is the Cornerstone himself, there is no problem. Examine pastoral demands according to His model and not people's expectations.

c. Christian people with good intentions can have unrealistic expectations. It is neither spiritual, wise, nor prudent to embrace demands on your time simply because they come from good Christian people. Examine the expectations of your parishioners. Accept legitimate requests based on God-placed priorities. Don't accept false guilt when you refuse to respond to inappropriate demands.

> It is neither spiritual, wise, nor prudent to embrace demands on your time simply because they come from good Christian people.

d. You can became a slave to the wrong master. Refuse to spend time and energy on things that don't make sense from an eternal perspective. Bathe each time commitment in prayer, asking for God's wisdom. Make the best decision you can make. Then, even when not well received, speak the truth in love (Eph. 4:15). Determine not to be in bondage to people or their expectations, even good people with legitimate-sounding expectations. Remember, you are Christ's bond servant, not theirs.

4. Allow the Holy Spirit to convict and empower.

Many of the issues in this book may make you recognize where you made poor choices. Make sure that you allow the Holy Spirit to do the convicting. Make sure that God's Word points to places where change needs to occur. However, even if the Holy Spirit has used this book to convict your heart, unless you appropriate His power to resolve the issues, it will make little difference.

5. As a ministry leader, model rest and peace.

I cannot overstate how important this issue is. Isaiah makes the same case when he says: "And the work of righteousness will be peace, and the service of righteousness, quietness and confidence forever" (32:17). While the prophetic meaning of this verse points to the millennial reign of Christ at the second coming of our Lord, there is also a temporal meaning. Isa. 32:17 reminds all Christian leaders that if we do "the work of righteousness," the work produces peace. If we do "the service of righteousness," the work produces quietness and confidence.

Unfortunately, the scores of pastors I have talked to experience a far different outcome than what Isaiah describes. For many, their ministry work results in more stress, exhaustion, ill health, and despair. Some work their way into disillusionment and bitterness.

That is why implementing a plan is crucial. That is why a plan to change must be as practical to implement as it is transformational to live. I offer the following strategies as a good way to get started. I want you to revolutionize the way you work and enjoy revolutionary results from your God-called ministry. At the end of this book, you will find the strategies in list form. Make a copy and post them where you will see them every day. Place a copy on your calendar. Give a copy to your spouse. I pray that you will find practical help so that you can experience the fulfillment of Isaiah's great promise: quietness and confidence, even in the midst of a stressful ministry!

PRACTICAL STRATEGIES

1. **Commit yourself to God's biblical plan for rest and renewal.**

a. Protect private time with the Lord each day. That's the first way to rest your body, mind, and spirit. Just as you pray for "daily bread," you need to pray for energy to do His will. That strength comes from daily quiet time with the Father. This day-by-day renewal is as important for health as occasional times away. You can't make up for the cumulative overload of daily stress by occasionally taking extra time off. Regularity is the key. Find the daily time and place that works for you. When you are quiet in God's presence, He will set you free from much of the stress and tension of daily living.

> You can't make up for the cumulative overload of daily stress by occasionally taking extra time off.

b. Rest one full day each week. Rest does not require immobility. Recreational rest often accomplishes the healing you need. However, **you must remove yourself from all ministry responsibilities.** For example, playing golf with a close friend can be very renewing. However, golfing with someone to help with spiritual needs is not rest. It's ministry! Do not try to get around the implications of God's command for weekly rest.

A wise pastor friend of mine named Jim models this lesson well. He pastored small churches in Arizona for his entire ministry. Although his churches were small, his influence was not. By compassion and a warm sense of humor, Jim led more young people to Christ in his churches and summer camps than anyone I have ever known. Jim loved golf, and he loved discipling young pastors. He also understood their tendency to overwork. Because of this, he often invited a pastor friend to golf with him on his day off. One morning he called an especially zealous young pastor. He said, "John, this is your buddy Jim. I need some 'counseling' out here on the golf course." When John said that he was too busy, Jim made one more appeal: "John, after you have your heart attack and go to heaven, just remember your buddy Jim, here, will still be leading people to Jesus and playing golf on his day off." John got the message and replied, "I'll be there in 30 minutes." I don't know what happened to John, but Jim pastored for 60 years. He led many people to Jesus and enjoyed much victory because he obeyed God in this and other ministry issues.

    c. Plan periodic times of renewal. Jesus models this strategy. One day He said to His disciples, "'Come away by yourselves to a lonely place and rest a while.' (For there were many people coming and going, and they did not even have time to eat.) And they went away in the boat to a lonely place by themselves" (Mark 6:31-32).

    I am sure that there are "many people coming and going" in your ministry as well. Jesus still invites: "Come away by yourselves to a lonely place and rest a while." Please listen to His call. Many pastors follow Jesus' example by taking two or three days per quarter for rest, prayer, and renewal with their spouse. Lay leaders do not resist. In fact, many encourage them to continue. They understand how much this benefits the church.

    d. Make your vacation a real vacation. These times are important for your family. Remember that they face a unique set of stresses because of your ministry. The whole family needs these extended times of recreation and rest. Do not mix ministry with time away during vacation. Don't use vacation time to be a conference speaker or to do research for sermon preparation. These times away should be some of your family's greatest memories. Don't take anything with you that will take your attention away from fun and family.

2. Do not underestimate how the body impacts the mind and spirit.

I doubt that many of you would compare yourselves to the great prophet Elijah. However, many Christian leaders have experienced the same kind of depression Elijah faced after his historic victory over the prophets of Baal. A careful look at this passage of Scripture reveals that Elijah was even suicidal! He says, "Now, O LORD, take my life" (1 Kings 19:4). After experiencing a great victory, how could such a dedicated believer take such a dive? How could someone be so depressed after witnessing one of God's most powerful exhibitions in all of history? How could God tolerate such faithlessness in someone who had experienced His sovereignty?

Let me make a medical aside. If I treated someone this despondent in my emergency department, medical protocol compels me to admit the person to psychiatric service. During this admission, the psychiatric medical team would closely observe the individual. They would also take required "suicidal precautions." Those are measures to prevent people from hurting or killing themselves. I make the point to illustrate that Elijah's depression was very serious.

But Elijah, instead of seeking medical intervention, experienced divine intervention. God responded to Elijah's emotional state, but He didn't rebuke, chastise, or punish. In fact, *God allowed Elijah to sleep first*. Later, He sent an angel with a meal and some water (vv. 5-6). It wasn't until after another complete cycle of sleep, food, and water that Elijah was ready for his journey and next assignment (vv. 6-8).

How could God tolerate depression and weakness in one who should have been stronger? Because *He understands how the body impacts the mind and spirit*. God understood that Elijah was sleep deprived, hypoglycemic (having low blood sugar), and dehydrated. God gave Elijah what he needed, not what he deserved! God knew that Elijah's body had limits. He knows that yours does too.

Perhaps you have been low, despondent, or depressed.

Don't expect to move through it by rebuking, chastising, or punishing yourself for weakness or apparent faithlessness. Accept physical and emotional limitations that God already understands. Then take a rest. Rest in His grace, in His compassion, and in His healing. Never forget that He loves you as much as He loved Elijah!

3. Mark regular days off and special days away on the calendar in advance.

This is not a trivial suggestion. The Bible clearly shows that time away is *not a worthless period when nothing of value happens.* These rest times are *appointments* with your Creator. That's why you should treat time away from your ministry as one of your most important appointments!

What would you do if Dr. James Dobson or Rev. Billy Graham offered to spend a day alone with you? Do you think that you would have time for one of these men on your calendar? Of course you would. Do you realize that Someone far more important wants time with you? Mark the appointment on your calendar. Then, don't let anyone or anything take God's time away from you.

Do not disturb. Meeting with God.

At a pastors' retreat, Dr. Ray Ortlund told of being stressed out early in his ministry. He testified, "My life was changed when I invited the Lord to look at my overbooked calendar. First, I blocked in my weekly day off. Then the Lord directed me to cancel some of the commitments that I had scheduled. Others I could not just drop." He went on to say, "It took time to simplify my life. But after this transition time, *I no longer placed anything on my calendar without prayerfully awaiting the Lord's approval.* He taught me that He could plan well in advance. Since I allowed the Holy Spirit to control my schedule, I have become more relaxed, more fulfilled, and more joyful."[1]

Take your days of rest as seriously as Jesus did. In fact, why don't you take time to look at your calendar right now? First, mark your weekly days off. Then schedule personal "wilderness" time for two to three days in the next several months. Write in the following reminder: *Do not disturb. Meeting with God.*

4. Get away from the phone on your day off.

As you review your ministry day, you will find that the phone enables you to do many important things without leaving your office. While the phone is time-effective in the office, it makes you overavailable away from church. This means that people will use the phone to reach you even when you need a break. For this reason, people may find it difficult to refrain from calling you on your day off. If a telephone ring instantly connects you back to your work, you cannot take the complete rest God wants you to have. Even if you are only pastoring by phone, you need a break.

I'm sure that many pastors fear missing an emergency in the church. However, there are technological advances that allow you to "call screen." Then, pick up the phone for *true emergencies.* Leave urgent issues for the next day, *after* your Sabbath rest is complete.

In the emergency department, I often have the responsibility for caring for 25 to 30 patients all at once. It is impossible to see them simultaneously. Ultimately, every need gets attention. But the person with bronchitis has to wait, sometimes a long time, when the man in the next room stops breathing, and a woman is delivering her baby in the hallway. In this environment, I have to develop a high threshold for considering something an emergency. Otherwise, I would spend all of my time running from one pseudoemergency to the next. People could die in the process. If I treated every urgent need as an emergency, I would delay addressing too many *true* emergencies. I could be fired!

Develop an emergency physician's threshold for defining an emergency. Very few people have emergencies by this definition. Most things can wait! This allows you to give immediate attention to the people and situations that truly need emergency attention without regularly robbing you of your time away.

5. Develop an accountability relationship with one or more wise counselors.

Accountability relationships are incredibly important to spiritual leaders. These friendships dramatically reduce the pressures that you face. Discuss your schedule and your responsibilities with these friends on a regular basis. An increasing number of pastors find great value in developing accountability partners. However, a few may be unwilling to subject their schedule to someone else's scrutiny. Face it. You need someone to ask you every week if you are taking your day off and what you will do with that day! While this is not the only subject for an accountability partner to evaluate, it is one of the important issues that should not be left out.

6. Talk with your spouse before adding any new responsibility.

No one wants you to succeed more than your spouse. Listening to your spouse in these matters will help you schedule work in ways that please God and protect your marriage and family.

There is another reason to have this discussion. When you involve your spouse in these decisions, your ministry mate is likely to own them with you. For instance, let's say someone asked you to serve on a board that requires out-of-town trips. You discuss it with your spouse, and both of you agree that this is a responsibility that God desires you to do. When the time comes for you to make the trip, your spouse is much more likely to view your absence in a positive light.

Of course, a spouse may also say no. In fact, it is likely that your mate will counsel you to reject more responsibilities than you would have rejected. Several pastors that I interviewed agreed that their spouses made more right decisions about schedule than they would have made. Is it possible that this is why many ministers fail to discuss responsibility loads with a spouse? It is this lack of interaction that causes much marital friction in the lives of today's pastors. You cannot fulfill your ministry calling independent of the person with whom you are one flesh. God designed marriage as a partnership. Your spouse has a right to be involved in your ministry decisions, especially those that impact both of your time.

7. Never give an immediate answer about new responsibilities.

It is nearly impossible to consider the full impact of a potential responsibility the first time you think about it. True emergency decisions are rare. Don't allow others to force you to make quick decisions when it comes to adding things to your responsibility list. In fact, if you find a situation or a person *demanding* an immediate answer, consider it a red flag. God rarely requires you to take on new responsibilities without preparing you for them. *Never* accept new responsibilities without concentrated and prayerful consideration. And *rarely* do it without the counsel of others.

When someone wants to add a responsibility to your already crowded schedule, *always* say, "I need to pray about this and talk with my spouse." Say it and mean it! This response puts the request in proper perspective. Most people relax their need for an immediate answer. It is always easier to say yes when someone catches you off guard or encourages you to answer immediately. However, an immediate answer gives you no time to find *God's* answer for each decision.

> There is no evidence in Scripture that God is more pleased with a wrong yes than a wrong no.

Too many Christian leaders believe that it is more spiritual to err on the side of saying yes. However, there is no evidence in Scripture that God is more pleased with a wrong yes than a wrong no. Learn how to ascertain what God wants you to do, and give Him time to tell you.

8. Inform lay leaders that you are changing your priorities.

If you are serious about changing habits of overwork and stress, people will notice the change. If you fail to communicate your plans with lay leaders, they may misunderstand. They may interpret the change as reducing your ministry com-

mitment. It would be an unfortunate paradox if people inter-
preted your plan to *prevent* burnout as evidence that you were
experiencing burnout! Hopefully, you can model effective
changes in a way to challenge your entire church to bring their
own personal schedules under God's control.

If you serve in a denominational structure,
you may find it wise to tell a superior about the
plan to reduce your overloaded schedule. They
can provide support and even mediation if
church members complain about your availability
changes.

**9. Frequently remind yourself that God doesn't
need you to save the world. He needs you to
obey!**

> **Nothing limits God's ability to carry out His plan to save the world more than disobedience.**

Nothing limits God's ability to carry out His
plan to save the world more than disobedience. Do not be an
accomplice to the enemy of God's eternal purpose. The days
are too treacherous and the time is too short to second-guess
God's sovereignty and His omniscience!

Begin to allow God to help you understand that, while
your ministry is important, it is only a minuscule part of the
history and scope of God's salvation plan for humanity. Look
for ways to let God do the saving while you do the obeying.

10. Get used to leaving unfinished business in ministry.

Most pastors have preached their own brand of harvest
messages from Luke 10:2: "The harvest is plentiful, but the laborers are few; therefore beseech the Lord of the harvest to
send out laborers into His harvest." However, I believe that few
understand the basic premise of this verse. The verse reminds
us that there are fewer harvesters when compared to the harvest's potential. The purpose of this verse is not to ask current
harvesters to work harder to make up the difference. Instead,
Jesus tells us to pray that *He* will send out more laborers.

And Jesus was speaking to His appointed leaders about
taking the salvation message to the whole world. He did not
command them to ask for more strength or gifts or even for a

greater harvest from their work. Rather, the leaders were simply to pray for more laborers.

Accept the fact that the harvest is too big and there aren't enough workers. Accept the fact that, even when you obey God's plan for your ministry, there will always be needs that you cannot meet. Do not relieve this tension by working harder! Rather, do what Jesus commanded you to do. Pray that the Lord of the harvest will send more laborers.

11. Equip the new workers God sends, and delegate ministry responsibilities to them.

It is the *whole* church's responsibility to minister to the needs of people. However, they cannot do what they do not know how to do. Train them. Mentor them. Ask a leader in training to accompany you on ministry calls. Share your vision. If you are not spending a significant amount of ministry time equipping others to do the work of the church, you are probably doing too much of the work yourself.

12. Do for your congregation what you need them to do for you.

Don't forget that you minister to many exhausted, worn-out laypeople. Members who are active in ministry cope with many of the same problems you wrestle with in your own life. Because of this, you need to alter your expectations of *their* ministry loads in the same way you need them to alter their expectations of *yours.* Don't make them pay the price of overwork for others' negligence. Teach them to obey God's call to rest in their own lives. Do not entice them to overwork.

> If you are not spending a significant amount of ministry time equipping others to do the work of the church, you are probably doing too much of the work yourself.

Remember, *all* disobedience compromises the kingdom of God. You cannot afford to be more comfortable with the disobedience of overwork than you are with the disobedience of irresponsibility or laziness. You must teach every church leader about the peace and rest Christ plans for them. And you must do more than that. You must model it.

13. Begin to plan a sabbatical now.

No matter how long you have been at your current pastoral assignment, consider preparing your church for a sabbatical. There has never been a time in the church when pastoral sabbaticals were so desperately needed. I realize that many pastors believe sabbaticals to be impractical or unattainable. As one point of hope, I would like to share a plan that my denominational district adopted in Arizona.

There are 60 churches organized within this district. Approximately two years ago, our district superintendent presented the pastoral sabbatical concept to district leadership. Each layman on this board of clergy and laity demonstrated genuine excitement about the concept.

A subcommittee developed a specific plan that encouraged all of the churches on our district to release their pastors for the following:

1. A full 24 hours off each week.
2. A week off every seven months.
3. A sabbatical of seven weeks after seven years of service to the local church.

Please understand that these times of rest do not qualify as "vacation." Nor does vacation time meet the needs of sabbatical. Vacation is earned as an employment benefit. The seventh rest cycles give time to God out of obedience, not reward.

The board left specific logistics for local church bodies and their pastors to work out. For example, it is up to the local churches to work out issues involving whether time spent in a previous church will qualify toward a sabbatical.

How have churches received this? After only two years, 14 of the 60 pastors on our district have either taken a sabbatical or plan to take one in the near future. It appears that many, if not most, will follow some form of the plan.

It wasn't easy to predict how churches, especially laymen, would respond to this progressive step. As a board, we were concerned that local church leadership might think that we were forcing them to comply with a plan they did not want. Instead, we found that support for the concept increased. In fact, I believe that many local churches now understand that following a seventh rest plan may prevent them from losing their pastor.

Today, pastors move from one church to the next on an average of every four years. In the past, the average was every seven years.[2] It seems that moving to the next church became a kind of *surrogate sabbatical*. As the complexities of ministry have increased, so has the frequency of these *surrogate sabbaticals*. However, if pastors would take true sabbaticals, I believe that relocation would occur far less frequently. This issue becomes more important in view of the fact that the greatest ministry effectiveness occurs in long pastorates.[3] Could it be that when churches refuse to give pastors real sabbaticals as opposed to surrogate ones, they prevent effective ministry? A sabbatical may be one of the most important things that you can do for yourself. It may also be one of the most important things that you can do for your church!

14. Set aside time for studying God's Word.

The Bible clearly teaches that the two most important jobs of the pastor are prayer and preaching the Word. Unfortunately, today's pastors neglect these two priorities more than their predecessors did.

The pastors I talk to, who are effective in their preaching, block out prolonged periods of time each week to study God's Word. Schedule this time first. Make this time inviolate. Do not use leftover time for sermon preparation. Also, resist the temptation to use your day off for sermon preparation. Sermon preparation is a part of your ministry task. Everything God wants you to do fits within six days of work.

> Everything God wants you to do fits within six days of work.

Not only is studying God's Word a primary part of your work, but also it is a key ingredient to the restful heart God wants you to have. God always gives rest to anyone who does

His will. Therefore, as you obey God with this priority, He will rest you in the middle of your busy assignment, even when this obedience excludes some secondary ministry tasks. He called you to preach; nothing else can replace this priority. Remember that "the work of righteousness will be peace, and the service of righteousness, quietness" (Isa. 32:17). If you want the peace and quiet, study and preach the Word diligently!

15. Develop a life of prayer.

There is no substitute for prayer. Godly leaders from the Bible spent large amounts of time in prayer. Jesus himself went *often* to the wilderness to pray. Paul commands us to "pray without ceasing" (1 Thess. 5:17). He said of himself and the other church leaders that "we night and day keep praying most earnestly" (3:10).

Daniel is another Bible character who demonstrated the importance of meaningful and unhurried times of prayer. When Daniel told Nebuchadnezzar his dream and its interpretation, it impressed the king to do the following: "Then the king promoted Daniel and gave him many great gifts, and he made him ruler over the whole province of Babylon and chief prefect over all the wise men of Babylon" (2:48).

Decades later, after the fall of the Babylonian Empire, Daniel was promoted into another position of great responsibility. King Cyrus of Persia had appointed Darius to be the regional governor ("king") of the Babylonian region of the empire. As King Darius developed his administration, the following happened: "Then this Daniel began distinguishing himself among the commissioners and satraps because he possessed an extraordinary spirit, and the king planned to appoint him over the *entire* kingdom" (6:3, emphasis added).

It is an understatement to say that Daniel was a busy man. He was the chief governmental administrator over two of the greatest civilizations of the world. With that in mind, review an event in his life that reveals that he did not allow his responsibilities to take away from his prayer life. The event occurred after Darius signed the document that prevented the people from praying to anyone except the king: "Now when Daniel knew that the document was signed, he entered his house (now in his roof chamber he had windows open toward Jerusalem); and he *continued* kneeling on his knees three times a day, praying and giving thanks before his God, *as he had been doing previously*" (v. 10, emphases added).

Nothing stopped Daniel from praying. Not a busy day. Not the king's decree. Even understanding that the injunction against prayer lasted for only 30 days didn't deter Daniel. Daniel understood that life without continuous prayer was not worth living! I don't know about you, but Daniel's life convicts me!

> **Daniel understood that life without continuous prayer was not worth living!**

Dr. Billy Kim, the pastor of one of the largest churches in the world, made this convicting statement: "As I look back over my ministry, if I had it to do over again, I would have preached less and prayed more."[4] This comes from a man who preaches to 60,000 people every Sunday. Looking back on his successful ministry, he says he would have preached less and prayed more! God's greatest leaders exhibit greatness, not because of their skills, but because of their praying.

Look again at the dispute between the Hellenistic Jews and native Hebrews in Acts 6:1-7. The primary reason for appointing seven men to serve tables was so that they could devote themselves "to *prayer*, and to the ministry of the word" (v. 4, emphasis added).

Do not underestimate your need for prayer. Overcoming issues of overwork and exhaustion in your life *begins* with a life devoted to prayer. Without prayer, all of the other strategies will fail!

16. Determine to obey today!

I believe that God wants us to learn to say no to requests for more work. We must do it even if people perceive the wrong thing about us. Educate people as you go, but don't base your obedience on other's positive reactions.

This is no time for partial obedience. Of course you have voiced some obedient noes in the past. However, most pastors that I talked to believed that they didn't say no enough. Some of these pastors went on to admit that even if they shouldn't be doing so much, they didn't plan any changes.

Saul's partial obedience caused catastrophic results. He lost his kingdom, he lost his authority, and he lost his life. Other biblical accounts chronicle similar tragedies from delayed obedience. The story of the freed Hebrews on the other side of the Red Sea miracle is one such example.

It was after the special reconnaissance team brought back the 10 to 2 report *against* taking possession of the Promised Land. Unfortunately, the word of the cowardly spies prevailed, causing Moses, Aaron, Joshua, and Caleb no small distress. They were nearly stoned for trying to convince the people to follow God's command to take possession of the land. Ultimately, Moses told the Hebrews that they could obey God and live in the Promised Land or obey the cautious report and die in the wilderness. Tragically, they refused to obey (Num. 14:30-34, 39).

However, during the night, an amazing thing happened. The people changed their minds and decided to obey God after all. "In the morning, however, they rose up early and went up to the ridge of the hill country, saying, 'Here we are; we have indeed sinned, but we will go up to the place which the LORD has promised'" (v. 40). However, Moses counseled the people against this decision with these words: "Why then are you *transgressing the commandment of the LORD,* when it will not succeed? Do not go up, lest you be struck down before your enemies, for the LORD is not among you. For the Amalekites and the Canaanites will be there in front of you, and you will fall by the sword, inasmuch as you have turned back from following the LORD. *And the LORD will not be with you*" (vv. 41-43, emphases added).

Unfortunately, the Israelites did not listen to Moses: The Amalekites and Canaanites defeated them (vv. 44-45).

What an incredible story! It began with Caleb telling them what God wanted them to do. When they grumbled, Moses, Aaron, and Joshua joined Caleb in trying to persuade them to take the land. When they rejected God's plan, Moses prophesied that all of the adults of that generation would die in the wilderness and that their children would have to wander for 40 years.

Having heard this prophecy, they mourned. After considering the words of Moses overnight, the Israelites decided to obey God's command to take Canaan. But now there was an unexpected hitch. When they told Moses that they were going to "obey" God, he told them that they must **Delayed obedience is disobedience!** *not* go into Canaan because God was no longer with them. Delayed obedience is disobedience! Just one day later, it was too late to obey! What God required in faith the day before became presumptuous disobedience on the next day. Why? Because the people wanted to obey God when *they* wanted to obey Him.

When God lays His plan upon your life, that is the best time to obey. Apply this clear message about obedience to these strategies to change patterns of overwork and stress. Heed the words from Hebrews you have no doubt preached from: "'TODAY IF YOU HEAR HIS VOICE, DO NOT HARDEN YOUR HEARTS, AS WHEN THEY PROVOKED ME.' For who provoked Him when they had heard? Indeed, did not all those who came out of Egypt led by Moses? And with whom was He angry for forty years? Was it not with those who sinned, whose bodies fell in the wilderness? And to whom did He swear that they should not enter His rest, but to those who were *disobedient?*" (3:15-18, emphases added).

The Last Word

We started with a ticking time bomb. We started with statistics revealing that too many pastors are leaving the ministry. While there are many reasons for this fallout, stress, ill health, disease, discouragement, and depression play a big part. We've examined medical research that demonstrates the undeniable link between stress, ill health, and disease. No matter how you interpret the bottom line from statistics and research, one fact surfaces: We have too many pastors paying the wrong price for giving their lives to ministry.

The good news is that God neither desires nor sanctions imbalance and burnout in order to make His kingdom come to earth. So why do we allow it? Every servant of God, clergy and laity, must submit to God whatever part of himself or herself that allows it, enables it, condones it, or does not correct it.

God neither desires nor sanctions imbalance and burnout in order to make His kingdom come to earth.

God wants to defuse this ticking time bomb. He wants to protect you from a devastating explosion. But He needs you to obey His clear command to practice sabbatical rest. He needs you to renew your priority commitment to prayer and preaching the Word. He needs you to address any lifestyle pattern that does not model His strength made perfect in your weakness. Each new commitment to obey protects effective ministry and defuses the time bomb.

What about you? Have you seen yourself in these pages? Have you identified a potential time bomb, even if an explosion does not seem to be in your immediate future? With the best of intentions, have you bought into the wrong model for ministry? It's time to change, to correct, and to return to the priorities that God uses to make His kingdom come to earth through your ministry.

As a physician, I write prescriptions. May I write one for you and deliver it as a prayer?

Dear God,

Rest Your weary servants from carrying any expectation that did not come from You.

Release Your called ones from any responsibility that You did not sanction.

Renew Your ministers as they obey Your command to practice Sabbath rest, regularly.

Rekindle their hunger and thirst for the work of righteousness so that their need for rest, peace, and confidence will be fully satisfied.

Demonstrate Your unfailing power to make strength come from submitted weakness.

Encourage them to address any lifestyle pattern that adversely affects their health, their marriage, their family, or their ability to minister Your way.

Defuse the time bombs that have the potential to destroy ministers and ministry in ways that will decrease the number of workers available to bring in Your harvest.

Refresh the ones You have called with a new awareness that You do not require unreasonable, imbalanced, or unhealthy service.

May this reader find Your rest today and in all the days of ministry to come.

In the name of the One
> *who went to the wilderness often*
> *to meet with His Father,*

In the name of Jesus,
> *our ministry Model and Enabler,*
> *Amen.*

STRATEGIES FOR DEFUSING THE TIME BOMB

▷ Commit yourself to God's biblical plan for rest and renewal.

- Protect private time with the Lord each day.
- Rest one full day each week.
- Plan periodic times of renewal.
- Make your vacation a real vacation.

▷ Do not underestimate how the body impacts the mind and spirit.

▷ Mark regular days off and special days away on the calendar in advance.

▷ Get away from the phone on your day off.

▷ Develop an accountability relationship with one or more wise counselors.

▷ Talk with your spouse before adding any new responsibility.

▷ Never give an immediate answer about new responsibilities.

▷ Inform lay leaders that you are changing your priorities.

▷ Frequently remind yourself that God doesn't need you to save the world. He needs you to obey!

▷ Get used to leaving unfinished business in ministry.

▷ Equip the new workers God sends, and delegate ministry responsibilities to them.

▷ Do for your congregation what you need them to do for you.

▷ Begin to plan a sabbatical now.

▷ Set aside time for studying God's Word.

▷ Develop a life of prayer.

▷ Determine to obey today!

▷ Prevent relational isolation.
- Take time to relate to your spouse on nonministry issues.
- Plan family activities that provide time to talk together.
- Find a pastor to be your prayer partner.
- Make close friendships with a few key laypersons in your congregation.
- Frequently remind yourself that close friendships are an important part of maintaining your health.
- Make a relationship circle.

▷ Prevent emotional baggage for yourself and your family by encouraging healthy grieving strategies.
- Bring healthy closure to key relationships.
- Take sufficient time off between pastorates.
- Give yourself permission to grieve in your new pastorate.
- Become familiar with the normal stages of grief to help you identify where you are in the cycle.
- Don't bury your feelings under work in your new ministry.

ENDNOTES

1. Ray Ortlund, quotation from message at a pastors' retreat, Three Rivers, Calif., 1984.

2. George Barna, *Today's Pastors* (Ventura, Calif.: Regal Books, 1993), 36.

3. Ibid., 37.

4. Billy Kim, quotation from message at the Promise Keepers Conference, Los Angeles, May 1995.